Mindsets in the Classroom

Building a Culture of Success and Student Achievement in Schools

Mary Cay Ricci

PRUFROCK PRESS INC.

WACO, TEXAS

Library of Congress Cataloging-in-Publication Data

Ricci, Mary Cay, 1960-
 Mindsets in the classroom : building a culture of success and student achievement in schools / by Mary Cay Ricci.
     pages cm
Includes bibliographical references.
ISBN 978-1-61821-081-4 (pbk.)
1. Learning, Psychology of. 2. Academic achievement. I. Title.
LB1060.R495 2013
370.15'23--dc23

                              2013017464

Edited by Lacy Compton

Cover and layout design by Raquel Trevino

ISBN-13: 978-1-61821-081-4

Printed in the United States of America.

At the time of this book's publication, all facts and figures cited are the most current available. All telephone numbers, addresses, and websites URLs are accurate and active. All publications, organizations, websites, and other resources exist as described in the book, and all have been verified. The authors and Prufrock Press Inc. make no warranty or guarantee concerning the information and materials given out by organizations or content found at websites, and we are not responsible for any changes that occur after this book's publication. If you find an error, please contact Prufrock Press Inc.

Prufrock Press Inc.
P.O. Box 8813
Waco, TX 76714-8813
Phone: (800) 998-2208
Fax: (800) 240-0333
http://www.prufrock.com

TABLE OF CONTENTS

Dedication

For my children—Christopher, Patrick, and Isabella.
You continue to inspire me. May you always believe that with
effort and perseverance you can do anything.

For my parents—Joe and Mary Ellen Marchione.
Thank you for believing in me.

For Enio—Thank you for your support and patience.
For the people in my professional life who saw things in me that I
did not see in myself—Ginny, Carl, and Monique.

CHAPTER 1

WHAT ARE MINDSETS, AND HOW DO THEY AFFECT THE CLASSROOM?

"Look at her paper—she's the smart one!" It was the first month of school in a third-grade classroom, and I was visiting the students to see if they had any prior knowledge about the brain. This particular school had a 70% poverty rate and the majority of students did not have English as their first language. As I circulated around the tables, I was observing a student writing copiously when I heard it: "Look at her paper—she's the smart one!" This announcement proudly came from one of her classmates. When I assured him that he along with his classmates were all working hard on the assignment, he agreed, but again shared that this particular classmate would have the best paper.

What I discovered in this classroom was a profound example of a fixed mindset at play—an 8-year-old child who believed that his classmate was the "smart one," and that no matter the amount of hard work he put in, her paper would always be better. In this case, the child didn't see that he, too, could be the "smart one" or have one of the "best papers" in his classroom, a mindset I have seen during my time as an educator and consultant often. That's where this book comes in—to help the many teachers, administrators, parents, and students like the one in this story realize that they can change the way they think about success and intelligence in the classroom.

Can Intelligence Be Changed? What Are Growth Mindsets and Fixed Mindsets?

The belief that intelligence is malleable and can be developed is not a new concept. However, the idea that intelligence can be changed and grown in both children and adults has seen more popularity in recent years thanks to the work of Stanford University professor of psychology, Dr. Carol Dweck, and her 2006 book, *Mindset: The New Psychology of Success*, which looks at the concept of "growth mindsets" and "fixed mindsets" among successful people as far-ranging as athletes Alex Rodriguez and John McEnroe, CEOs Lou Gerstner and Ken Lay, and teachers Marva Collins and Rafe Esquith. Dweck's research and development of the fixed and growth mindset theory has also contributed to a major shift in thinking about student learning and intelligence.

Dweck (2006) described a belief system that asserts that intelligence is a malleable quality and can be developed—a *growth mindset*. Learners with a growth mindset believe that they can learn just about anything. It might take some struggle and some failure but they understand that with effort and perseverance, they can succeed. The focus of a growth mindset individual is on learning, not on looking smart. An educator with a growth mindset believes that with effort and hard work from the learner, all students can demonstrate significant growth and therefore all students deserve opportunities for challenge. Add to this belief an effective teacher armed with instructional tools that differentiate, respond to learner's needs, and nurture critical thinking processes, and you have a recipe for optimum student learning.

> ### growth mindset
> a belief system that suggests that one's intelligence can be grown or developed with persistence, effort, and a focus on learning

Dweck also presents a different belief system about intelligence; the belief that intelligence is something you are born with and the level of intelligence cannot be changed—*a fixed mindset*. A person with a fixed mindset might truly believe that he has a predetermined amount of intelligence, skills, or talents. This belief system is problematic at both ends of the continuum. For those students who struggle or do not perceive themselves as smart, it becomes a self-fulfilling prophecy. Because they don't really believe that they can be successful, they will often give up and not put forth effort. For those students who are advanced learners, they can become consumed with "looking smart" at all costs. They may have coasted through school without really putting forth much effort, yet they are often praised for their good grades and strong skills. Often, an advanced learner with a fixed mindset will start avoiding situations where she may fail; she can become "risk adverse." In her book, Dweck (2006), using tennis star John McEnroe as an example, noted that a person with a fixed mindset often is a high achiever who blames outside forces when he or she "fails" at a task.

> ### fixed mindset
> a belief system that suggests that a person has a predetermined amount of intelligence, skills, or talents

Think for a minute about your own mindset. A mindset is a set of personal beliefs and is a way of thinking that influences your behavior and attitude toward yourself and others. An educator's mindset directly influences how a child feels about him or herself and how he or she views him- or herself as a learner. A child's mindset directly affects how he or she faces academic challenges. A child with a growth mindset perseveres even in the face of barriers. A child with a fixed mindset may give up easily and not engage in the learning process.

A fixed or growth mindset can directly affect family dynamics as well. It is not surprising to note that parents also have a big impact on how children view themselves. They will often view their children through specific lenses: "Joseph was born knowing his math facts," "Domenic has always asked good questions," and "Catherine just knows how to interpret a piece of literature." These are all examples of a fixed mindset, even though the statements sound positive. These statements describe who these children "are," not the effort that they have put forth. As educators, think of some occasions when you have heard a parent describe her child in a way that rationalizes perceived weaknesses: "She is just like me; math was not my thing either" or "I can understand why he does not do well in reading; I never liked to read." (Ideas and resources for helping parents embrace a growth mindset will be discussed in Chapter 6.)

Shifting Mindsets

Breaking down the belief that intelligence is static can be a challenge, but with the proper groundwork and education, little by little a mindset can shift. Expecting a shift in mindset immediately is not realistic; after all, some educators have had a fixed mindset belief for most of their lives. Even after someone has had a self-proclaimed mindset shift, she will need to make a conscious effort to maintain that belief.

A fixed mindset has an elasticity that continually wants to spring back. For example, a twice-exceptional child (a gifted student with learning disabilities) called to share a college schedule with his mother who also happened to be an educator. The parent had a mindset "shift" several years ago and had proudly told me all she did to encourage a growth mindset culture within their home. The schedule her son shared involved 8 a.m. classes and a course roster that included macroeconomics, international business, accounting, analysis of media, and management. His mother noted that the fixed mindset mentality buried within her wanted to scream, "Are you crazy? You are setting yourself up for failure!" Instead, she responded, "It sounds like a challenging schedule, and I know that with continued effort, you will be able to manage it." Believing that all children can, with effort, persistence, and motivation succeed, is the heart of this belief.

Brain-Based Research

One of the reasons for this shift in thinking about intelligence is due to the available technology that examines the function and make-up of the brain. Recent brain research negates the notion that intelligence is "fixed" from birth. Formal and informal studies demonstrate that the brain can develop with the proper stimulus. Other current research in neuroscience emphasizes the concept of neuroplasticity. Neuroplasticity is the ability of the brain to change, adapt, and "rewire" itself throughout our entire life. Anyone who has ever witnessed someone recovering from a stroke has had a front row seat in watching neuroplasticity. In the case of a stroke, for most patients, the brain begins the rewiring process almost immediately so that patients learn to speak and become mobile again. (However, it takes the hard work and effort put forth in therapy for stroke patients to fully regain what they've lost.) Neuroplasticity works both ways; it creates new connections and eliminates connections that are not used very often.

neuroplasticity
the ability of the brain to change, adapt, and "rewire" itself throughout our entire life

Understanding and believing in neuroplasticity is an important part of a growth mindset belief. Malcolm Gladwell, author of *Outliers: The Story of Success*, related the idea of neuroplasticity back to academic success when he discussed how some children are at a disadvantage academically simply because they don't have the opportunities to learn at the same levels of their peers during the summer months. He shared the following,

> It turns out that summer vacation is a massive disadvantage for poorer kids. Richer kids get a lot of help over the summer. Their homes are filled with books and things that advance their knowledge; they go to camp and have all these other activities. But a poor family can't do that. To improve that, we as a society would have to provide it in the first place. During the school year, poor kids actually outlearn richer kids. Then they stall over the summer. (Newman, 2008, para. 5)

This is an example of how neuroplasticity eliminates or weakens connections—in this case, the connections go unused for the children whose families cannot afford academic programming during the summer while the students who are provided with such opportunities during the summer can maintain their learning.

We now know so much more about the neurological aspects of the brain that it cannot help but inform the way we approach learning, instruction, and motivation. It directly affects teachers' beliefs and expectations about student potential and achievement. It is when educators and children (as well as their parents) learn about the brain and all of its potential and when they witness the impact that it has on learning that mindsets can begin to shift (see Chapter 8 for a discussion of how you can teach children about the brain).

Intelligence and Measuring Intelligence

Is it possible to increase your IQ? The University of Michigan partnered with the University of Bern to conduct a study that looked at the possibility of increasing IQ. This 2008 study (see Palmer, 2011) required participants to continually play a computerized memory game that involved remembering visual patterns. Each time a different pattern appeared, the participants heard a letter from the alphabet in their headphones. They were asked to respond when either the visual pattern on the screen or the letters they were hearing in their headphones were repeated. The time between the repeating of patterns and letters became longer as the game became more difficult. The researchers found that as the participants had practice and got better at the game, scores on IQ-style tests increased (Palmer, 2011).

This research and other studies like it contribute to the understanding of malleable intelligence, a key factor in growth mindset and a concept many educators struggle to understand. In general, educators do not have a lot of background in cognitive science. I recently asked several groups of educators, "What do cognitive abilities tests/IQ tests measure?" Without exception, there was hesitancy in responding to the question; after giving sufficient wait time, a few responses were shared: "a child's capability," "how smart they are," and "their innate ability." What surprised me more than their responses was the observation that so many of these teachers and administrators just could not answer the question. There are many times that educators are in situations where data is shared about a student, and that data often includes cognitive scores from gifted and talented screening processes, special education screening processes, and/or IQ tests. Who knew so many educators really have no idea what these assessments actually measure?

Cognitive ability tests measure *developed* ability. Therefore, if a child has never had an opportunity to develop reasoning processes, the outcome of one of these assessments would not be noteworthy. David Lohman (2002), professor of educational psychology at the University of Iowa and cocreator of the Cognitive Abilities

Test (CogAT), stated that abilities are developed through experiences "in school and outside of school" (para. 3). When parents and educators review these "intelligence" scores, assumptions may be made about the child and beliefs may kick in that place limits on the child's potential.

The Role of Potential and Hard Work

Potential. What a great word. It is all about possibilities. However, "potential" is often used in ways that can make me uncomfortable. Think of the phrase, "He is not working to his full potential" or "We will help your child reach his full potential." How does potential become "full"? Is it something that can be checked off on a report card? Potential can never be "full"; it is never-ending and our possibilities are infinite. As a person grows, learning and experiences become more sophisticated and challenging, growth continually occurs, and potential is never reached because it is impossible to reach. Perhaps many thought Michael Phelps reached his "full" potential after his 10th Olympic medal in 2008—a feat he went on to shatter at the 2012 Olympics when he won eight more medals. Believing that intelligence, talent, skills, and, yes, even athletic ability can be developed encourages these endless possibilities.

We are all born with potential. However, we might have innate strength or capacity in one or more specific areas. These strengths can manifest themselves in many ways. Strengths can be shown physically, creatively, socially, academically, perceptually—the possibilities are endless. Every child has strengths, and some children are born with a greater degree of specific strengths compared to their peer group. For those children with outstanding specific strengths or those who are identified as "gifted," their strengths deserve to be further developed. However, it is also important to consider that other children have the potential to work side-by-side or even surpass those with intrinsic abilities.

Think of a time that it took you a little longer to learn a new skill. It may have been something that required physical coordination, playing a musical instrument, using a new piece of technology, or learning a new instructional strategy. Then, once you learned this new skill, it became a strength for you. In fact, you surpassed many others who have had this skill for years. As an adult, you had the drive, motivation, and persistence to decide that reaching this goal was important to you. No one took away the opportunity to let you learn, no one told you it was "too hard" for you, no one told you that this was "not the right group" for you. No one put up barriers to hinder your learning.

Yet, sometimes our education system does all of the above. Our school structures eliminate opportunities, communicate low expectations, and prematurely remove students from challenging environments. Many reasons exist for hampering student potential in this way; one major obstacle is how we judge both adults and children by the speed in which things are completed.

Our society has become one that values pace. The faster, the better. If we don't get our medium, decaf, skim, extra hot, caramel latte in less than 2 minutes, then we are annoyed. If our Internet connection is not instant, then we grumble or click fast and furiously. If a driver in front of us is not going at a pace we agree with, then we use the horn or moan out loud. If an educator describes a bright child in their classroom or school, then we might hear him refer to the child as "quick" and those in the bottom reading group as "slow."

We need to step back, take a breath, and realize that it is not about how fast students master learning. It is about the persistence and effort that they put forth.

Growing School Communities That Embrace a Growth Mindset

Developing ways to establish a school community that promotes the belief that intelligence is malleable is the major goal of this book. The entire school staff— administrators, teachers, support staff—as well as parents must truly believe that all children can be successful. At the same time, children must also accept this belief system. Recall the vignette that opened this chapter—did the little boy who believed his classmate was the smartest embrace the idea that he too could be successful? Not so much, even with my prompting. Can you imagine how his attitude may have been different in this situation if he did ascribe to the belief that all children have the potential to experience success?

It is all about beliefs and expectations. One way that contributes greatly to both children and adults embracing this belief system is by learning about the brain and all of its possibilities (again, see Chapter 8 for learning tasks that both children—and adults!—can take on to learn more about the brain). Neuroscience has grown by leaps and bounds in the last several years and educating ourselves and our students about the brain has a huge impact on student effort and motivation.

Why Mindset Matters in Schools

Carol Dweck (2010) conducted a study of middle school math students in New York City. The students showed positive growth when they believed that intelligence is malleable and when they learned about their brains. Studies have shown that many students enter middle school with the belief that we are all born with a specific, set-in-stone intelligence level or a fixed mindset (Dweck, 2010). Similarly, it was shared with me that in one Washington, DC, suburban school working on changing its students' mindsets, it was determined through student feedback and interviews that more than 60% of the children entering grade 6 believed that they were born with specific academic strengths and weaknesses and that they could not change. *Based on this statistic,* I asked myself, *at what point do children transition to this kind of mindset?*

This prompted me to undertake my own studies. I began collecting data in kindergarten classes. In the fall, kindergarten students were surveyed to capture their beliefs about intelligence. In the two classrooms I surveyed—a classroom made up of high-poverty, diverse students and one with primarily middle-class students—100% percent of the children demonstrated a growth mind-

Table 1

Changes in Fixed and Growth Mindsets Across Grade Levels

Grade	Fixed Mindset	Growth Mindset
K	n/a	100%
1	10%	90%
2	18%	82%
3	42%	58%

set. They came to school in kindergarten thinking that they could learn and be successful. They were enthusiastic, full of promise, and ready to absorb social and intellectual knowledge!

With that optimistic data in hand, I moved on to a first-grade classroom; again, students were surveyed to capture their thinking about intelligence. In this case, only 10% of students in the first-grade class demonstrated a fixed mindset. For the most part, these first graders replicated the enthusiasm of the kindergarten students with the exception of only a few students who felt that some students were born smarter than others and that we cannot really change how smart we are. Time to move on to second grade. In these classrooms, I discovered that 18% of students demonstrated a fixed mindset. Are you beginning to see a pattern? With every increase in grade, more and more students believed that intelligence was a fixed trait: They agreed with the notion that "Some people are smart, some people are not." But perhaps the most surprising result was the large jump between second and third grade. Of the third-grade students I surveyed, 42% had a fixed mindset! Table 1 displays these findings.

This data sends a message loud and clear: We need to start working with educators and children as early as possible so they can maintain a belief system that communicates that all students can succeed. Our children walk into the school building on the first day of kindergarten ready to learn, believing in themselves with all of the optimism a 5-year-old can muster. We need to capture and sustain that mindset as they make their way through school. Now, how can we accomplish this?

CHAPTER 2

WHAT ARE SOME WAYS TO BEGIN BUILDING A GROWTH MINDSET SCHOOL CULTURE?

> "I can learn and get smarter even when work is hard."—Grade 4 student

The first stop along the path to building a growth mindset culture is to begin to build a school culture that values intellectual growth with a staff who has internalized the belief that intelligence can be cultivated. Ideally, every adult in the building must work toward adopting a mindset where he or she believes that with effort, motivation, perseverance, and the right menu of teaching strategies all students can achieve great things. School secretaries, building service workers, classroom aides, as well as teachers and administrators, should all commit to contribute to a growth school climate.

Professional development for all school personnel is the initial step toward this goal. It is important to first determine what belief systems are held by staff at the present time.

Whether you are working independently toward this goal, with a grade level team, an entire staff, or school system, it is important to begin by reflecting about your own personal belief system regarding intelligence. Suggestions for professional development can be found on the following pages. In addition, I have developed a comprehensive training plan for schools to use that can be found in Appendix A.

Step 1: Reflect and Preassess

Prior to a series of professional development sessions, teachers from a high-poverty, urban school district on the East Coast were asked to write down what they believed about intelligence using the worksheet in Figure 1.

These teachers' classrooms ranged from preschool through high school, with a wide spectrum of experience in education. Responses were varied and revealed many different opinions about intelligence. Teachers with a fixed mindset (who needed to change in their belief systems about intelligence) had responses like the following:

- "Intelligence is something you are born with (or not) and it's an unchangeable part of you."
- "It is innate and hereditary."
- "Intelligence does not change much throughout the lifetime, IQ stays roughly the same from age 8."
- "Intelligence is a student's ability to intake information, retain it, and regurgitate it at any given time."

Collecting and analyzing these responses served as a preassessment for me as a consultant; the goal was to capture their thinking prior to a series of workshops promoting malleable intelligence and then ask them to respond to the same question at the end of the workshop series. (Preassessment also models the first step required in planning for differentiated instruction, which will be addressed more completely later in this book.) I found that roughly one third of these teachers demonstrated a mindset where they believed that intelligence can be developed and two thirds held a belief that

---

Please share your beliefs about intelligence and/or what you were taught about student intelligence as you prepared to become a teacher.

My beliefs about intelligence are:

_____

_____

_____

_____

_____

Upon completion, put this in an envelope and put your name and today's date on the front of the envelope.

Later in the year, open the envelope and look at the response you wrote today. Reflect on any changes in your response.

Figure 1. Teacher worksheet for gauging personal beliefs about intelligence among students.

---

intelligence is fixed and stagnant, just like those quoted above. Interestingly, no pattern existed among the age or grade level of the students they taught, however, slightly more of the less-experienced teachers tended to have a growth mindset, while the more experienced teachers held a fixed mindset. (This difference also may have been due to when they completed their teaching degree coupled with neuroscience beliefs at that time. Perhaps the more-experienced teachers finished their degrees during the time when the "bell curve" mentality was more present and widely ascribed to in teacher education; this theory purported that there would always be students who were at the low end who could only go so far.)

A similar process can be conducted in your own school to see how your teachers feel about intelligence. Ideally, teachers should reflect and respond to the statement, "My beliefs about intelligence . . ." privately, seal their responses in an envelope, and at the end of the professional development series, compare their present mindset to their initial mindset.

After these individual reflections are complete, ask the staff members if they agree or disagree with the following statements that were adapted from Carol Dweck's (2006) work:
- Our intelligence is one of our fundamental traits.
- We can all learn new things, but we cannot really change how smart we are.

Assess the responses to see who agrees or disagrees with these statements. Educators might agree with both of these statements if they were taught or were raised to believe that intelligence cannot change.

Step 2: Educate Staff About the Malleability of the Brain

Some educators will resist the belief that all students can master high standards and that "gifted" behaviors can be developed. As I mentioned previously, this can be due in a large part to how the teachers and administrators have been educated. Many college and university teacher prep programs nourish the bell curve mentality of intelligence. Future teachers learn that a typical classroom will contain students at the "top" in the "middle" and at the "bottom." Does that always have to be the case? Can all students reach mastery? Can all students exceed grade-level expectations? Not everyone can be an Albert Einstein, Steve Jobs, Oprah Winfrey, or Hillary Clinton, but these people did not become who they were without much effort and perseverance.

Using the data you collected from Step 1, begin to plan ways to educate staff about theories of malleable intelligence. It is important to be aware that this will be a very new way of thinking for some educators, so be sensitive in the delivery of the message. Remember, many people believe that intelligence is an innate, permanent attribute that we are born with.

One analogy that can be made when communicating this change of thinking is to ask teachers to think about how a toothache is treated. Fifty years ago, when someone had a toothache, how was it treated? Most likely, the tooth was pulled. Today, because of advanced learning in the field of dentistry as well as new technological possibilities, more options are available. It is important to use examples such as this to give educators an "out" when learning about the possibilities of cultivating intelligence.

In Guy Kawasaki's 2011 book, *Enchantment: The Art of Changing Hearts, Minds, and Actions*, he described two kinds of people in the world:

> Eaters and bakers. Eaters want a bigger slice of an existing pie; bakers want to make a bigger pie. Eaters think that if they win, you lose, and if you win, they lose. Bakers think that everyone can live with a bigger pie. (p. 33)

Just like the bakers, all students can win without the existence of "losers" in the class. The "bigger pie" in this case is a growth mindset culture in the classroom.

It has been my experience that some teachers feel guilty after learning that intelligence can be developed. In the past, these teachers may have grouped and instructed students according to perceived intelligence or lowered expectations for some children for the same reason. Let educators know that it is because of new studies and scientific brain research that we now think differently about children and their potential, so they should not feel guilty about past practices. Instead, they can and should look forward—a growth mindset can be cultivated and shifted from a fixed belief.

Using the information that you learned from your preassessment, collaboratively plan multiple professional development sessions over several months. Share recent research about developed intelligence as well as the outcomes and educational implications based on the research. Using Dweck's (2006) terms of "fixed" and "growth" is entirely up to the individual school or system. You can also refer to the concepts as malleable, developed, or flexible intelligence (growth) or static, stationary, or stagnant intelligence (fixed).

Some schools chose to adopt a school motto, "We can all get smart at Harmony Park," or "Our Effort Is the Best at Havencrest." Understanding conceptually and communicating that intelligence is not a stagnant, innate attribute is the most important aspect of professional development. It is not important what specific researcher, book, or study this idea is built upon. The important thing is to just get the conversation started! One way to get staff thinking about this concept is by asking a few of the following discussion questions:

- Do we, as a society believe in or demonstrate a growth mindset? Why or why not?
- In what areas, personal or professional, do you have a fixed mindset? Why?

Many teachers have cited the following examples as areas in which they have a fixed mindset about their weaknesses or areas that they "will never be good at": technology, cooking, managing finances, sports. After teachers share some of the areas where they may have a fixed mindset, pose this question: "If you were given appropriate instruction and you had the time, persistence, and motivation, could you become a better cook? Money manager? Third baseman?" Of course they can, they'll answer. Then ask, "What if you wanted to learn to sing like Andrea Bocelli or Celine Dion? Well, you may or may not reach that goal, but with the proper instruction, much practice and effort, as well as motivation, could you become a better singer?" Yes, they'll likely answer. Most of us hold a fixed mindset in some aspects of our lives and so we sit on a continuum between "Of course I can do that!" and "I could never do that!" Providing everyday examples like these help teachers apply the concepts of malleable intelligence more easily.

Another way to introduce teachers to the idea of mindset is to talk about how one's emotions can be changed based on one's thinking, attitude, and behaviors. Andrew Weil, a doctor, and author of the 2011 book *Spontaneous Happiness: A New Path to Emotional Well-Being*, pointed to studies that show not only that can intelligence be developed, but emotions such as happiness and empathy can be developed as well. In the same way that practice improves a singer's voice, an athlete's performance, or a mathematician's growth and development, practice can also help a person become happier. Weil (2011) cited studies of the brain organized by Richard Davidson, Director of the Laboratory for Affective Neuroscience at the University of Wisconsin-Madison, that have shown that "There are no peaceful molecules without peaceful thoughts" (p. 65). Davidson performed brain scans on Matthieu Ricard, a Frenchman who attained a doctorate in molecular genetics, then later became a Buddhist monk. Based on data collection Davidson completed, he dubbed Ricard "The World's Happiest Man." What he found was that Ricard had increased activity in the left prefrontal cortex, which is associated with a positive emotions. Ricard makes an effort to be happy, practices happiness, and works to eliminate negative emotions through meditation—remember he is now a Buddhist monk! This study demonstrates that happiness can be learned with specific practice and effort.

In 2011, The Hawn Foundation collaborated with Scholastic to develop the MindUP curriculum (see http://thehawnfoundation. org/mindup), which focuses on the development of mindful attention to oneself and others. One component of this curriculum is developing optimism in our students: "We can train our brain to have an optimistic perspective, thanks to neuroplasticity" (Hawn Foundation, 2011, p. 111). In one study of the MindUp program, students self-reported improved optimism and self-control, with 82% of fourth- and fifth-grade students reporting a more positive outlook, 81% noting that they learned how to make themselves happier, and 56% suggesting they tried to help others more often after going through the program (Schonert-Reichl & Lawlor, 2010; Schonert-Reichl et al., 2011).

The MindUp resources suggest teaching students to use "self-talk" to practice positive thinking and to share with students the benefits of practicing optimism (the Jonsson School blog, a school that actively uses the MindUp curriculum, offers many examples of how MindUp can be used directly with students at http://brain-childblog.com/category/mindup). Being an optimistic learner is beneficial for students, as it helps them become ready to master new learning and be optimistic about their ability to do so. Remember Chapter 1's discussion of neuroplasticity? It is because of the brain's neuroplasticity that we have the ability to become happier, a concept that many teachers will grasp and be able to reapply to the idea of flexible intelligence.

Step 3: Educate Staff About Praise for Students

How do we praise our students? Walking through almost any school, you can hear teachers praise student success, behaviors, and attitudes. Educators must be more aware of the way we praise students if we are journeying down the path of a growth mindset school culture. Carol Dweck and her colleagues have presented sound evidence about the value of praising effort rather than outcome. Dweck (2006) has discovered through her research that students who believe that intelligence is something you are born with and cannot change are overly concerned about looking smart. This is particularly true with gifted and highly able students.

Therefore, praise such as "You are so smart" could be detrimental for students who hold a fixed belief about intelligence. Saying "You are so smart" is the equivalent of saying "You are so tall"—what did a child have to do with being tall? It is just a genetic trait that the child had no control over. Both praise statements recognize no action that the child has put forth. No effort is recognized. When adults praise what a child "is," such as tall or smart, the children attribute their accomplishment to a fixed trait they were born with. When adults praise actions or tasks that children "do," the children attribute accomplishment to their own effort. Often it is just a matter of adding on to the praise that is already stated. For example, if a teacher says, "You did a great job on that paper," she might add, "I can tell you worked very hard." Modifying or adding effort praise is all it takes to send a growth mindset message. Adults must also be aware of the nonverbal messages that they are sending to students. Folded arms, a stern face, a heavy sigh, or a roll of the eyes does not send a growth mindset message, no matter what words are coming from a person.

It is important to note that some gifted and highly able students believe that putting forth a lot of effort is a sign of weakness. If they have constantly been told that they are gifted and/or smart, they think that learning should be easy for them; therefore, they think that if you have to work hard, you must not be smart. David Sousa (2009), author of *How the Gifted Brain Learns*, finds that "children who are praised for their intelligence learn to value performance, while children praised for their effort and hard work value opportunities to learn" (p. 34).

Schools should provide professional development sessions for all adults in the building that focus on ways to praise students who value and promote growth. It is also important to put in place a support system that can provide feedback to staff. Peer coaching or school leadership can provide constructive feedback to all staff.

Step 4: Educate Teachers About the Brain

It is rare that I run into an educator who has had coursework or has independently read about the brain and its implications for learning. This goes back to that first question we asked educators to reflect on, "What is intelligence?" Many educators think they know enough about the brain, they may think that some children's brains are "quicker" and others "slower." The truth is that neuroscience is a field that is constantly changing and keeping up with all of the studies and research requires a commitment to do so. Even though the field of neuroscience is complex, basic conceptual understanding of the brain is simple and important for teachers as well as students.

In a nutshell: Neurons make new connections when you learn something new. These connections become stronger with practice and effort. The more connections, the denser your brain is. The more density, the "smarter" you are. (So, if you have ever been accused of being dense, that is a good thing!) Educators should have a clear understanding that these neural connections or pathways become stronger every time they are used. Picture brand new learning experiences as neurons being connected by a thin piece of thread. Every time that new learning is practiced and applied, that thin thread

21

becomes stronger and stronger until the learning is mastered. Now, that weak, thin piece of thread has the strength of a thick, strong, rope. In order to strengthen these neural connections for students, it is important for teachers to constantly make connections to prior knowledge and experiences. The more connections that are made during a learning sequence, the more physical changes occur in the brain by developing and strengthening neural paths. (Sample learning tasks for students can be found in Chapter 8.)

Both educators and students must recognize that a new neural pathway is like walking through an unexplored forest for the first time. The more frequently the path is used, the fewer the barriers and obstacles that stand in the way. Eventually a clear path is created. That new path represents a clear understanding of the content being taught.

Step 5: Teach Students About the Brain

Neuroscience is not a typical area of study in elementary and middle school curriculum and not often found in high school science with the exception of a chapter or unit embedded in biology classes. So how do educators find the time to teach students about their brain? Probably one of the most important things to realize is that this is not about just teaching a few lessons. It is an area that must be revisited and built upon over time. It is about introducing and explicitly teaching students, then routinely revisiting the concept of malleable intelligence so that students realize that intelligence is not about a fixed number, a grade on a paper, or a report card. Students must understand that intelligence is constantly changing based on effort, persistence, and motivation. They will soon realize that intelligence is something that grows as you use it and languishes if you don't.

More and more studies are surfacing about the importance of teaching neuroscience. In 2012, Marshall and Comalli published their study, "Young Children's Changing Conceptualizations of Brain Function: Implications for Teaching Neuroscience in Early Elementary Settings" in the *Early Education and Development*

journal. Their work consisted of a two-part study of children ages 4–14. The goal of the first part of the study was to determine what exactly these children already knew about the brain. The results indicated that the vast majority of these children believed that the brain's functions are limited to intellectual activity. In other words, they believed it is strictly used for thinking. Based on these results, a second study was conducted that determined that this very narrow view of brain function could be broadened even with brief classroom instruction. In this case, lessons were designed to teach kids about the brain's broader involvement with their five senses, physical activity, and everyday actions. This study found that even with a brief classroom lessons, first-grade students became significantly more aware of their brain's involvement with all of their senses rather than maintaining the narrow view of "My brain helps me think."

Step 6: Educate Parents

Over the last several years I have done many workshops for educators, as well as parents, on the topic of malleable intelligence and growth mindset. It is often a wake-up call for many of the parents I work with when I begin discussing the importance of having a growth mindset and not looking at their children through a lens of perceived intelligence. At the conclusion of these parent workshops, I take a few moments and ask parents to reflect on what they just heard. They are asked to jot down what they are thinking and what they are planning as a result of the presentation. Many are reflective about the way they speak to their kids. For example, one parent shared,

> I am planning on starting to make changes tomorrow morning during "morning rush." Instead of saying, "You're so slow" or "You're such a slow-poke," I will say "I really appreciate the effort that you put forth to get to school on time." I need to make a lot of changes.

It is also interesting to note that in almost every workshop, a parent asks, "Well, do the teachers know about this?" More ideas for parents can be found in Chapter 6.

The Final Step: Monitor, Evaluate, and Review School Protocols

If you are in a position where you have spent a good amount of time and training toward building a growth mindset culture, then it is now time to evaluate how well you, your school, or your district is doing. How do you monitor and make sure that, in fact, the building staff is working toward this every day? One way is to establish Look-Fors, student and teacher behaviors that you will observe when you walk through any room in the school building. These behaviors should evidence the building of a growth mindset belief. (Sample Look-Fors can be found in Chapter 9.) Another option is to utilize Professional Learning Communities (PLCs). These groups should focus discussion around the progress toward a growth mindset culture. Set up alerts online so leaders of PLCs will be notified when new articles or studies are released that focus on neuroscience in education and growth mindset. Have the PLCs adopt books like Dweck's or other popular titles (there are many listed in the Resources section) as book studies or book club selections. Reflecting on these readings together will help the groups change the way they think about intelligence.

Think about how students are placed in instructional groups and classes. Does the current student placement system contribute to a growth culture within the school? The following is an actual exchange of e-mails between a parent of an incoming ninth-grade student and the English department chair at the student's receiving high school. Read this exchange through the lens of a growth mindset. (Names and specific details have been changed or omitted in order to protect the guilty!)

Dear English Department Chair,

We are thrilled that our daughter, Emma, will be attending Great Hills High School next year. We wanted to share with you some information about her interest in literature. During her eighth-grade year, her love of literature has exploded! This is due, in part, to a great literature experience she has had this year. We have seen Emma dive deeply into the symbolism of each book she reads—she asks questions, interprets, analyzes characters' words and actions, foreshadows, and wants to discuss each and every book that she reads. Her writing has also shown great improvement over the last few months. We are thrilled about her newfound passion for literature. Standardized testing does not reflect this surge of interest, motivation, and achievement in the area of reading with meaningful interpretation. We are wondering what steps need to be taken in order to have her placed in freshman-level honors literature. She has maintained an A in Reading so far this year.

Emma has adopted a strong growth mindset in the area of literature, and she feels strongly that she can succeed in an honors literature class. We obviously do not want to see this growth and enthusiasm diminish in her. Please let us know what the process is for making this request. Thank you for your time and I look forward to hearing from you.

Sincerely,
Mr. and Mrs. M

The response back to the parents:

Dear Mr. and Mrs. M,

Thank you so much for your recent inquiry as to the feasibility of effecting a class placement change for your daughter, Emma. Placement is determined by the department chairs and in some cases consultation with other school staff. It is based on the candidate's performance on the placement test. We do take into consideration the candidate's grades in English and Reading as well (when a candidate is on the cusp of our cut-off criteria), but given the varied levels of preparedness of students coming from many different feeder schools, the scores do offer us the best method of determining the appropriate placement of the incoming students. The cut-off for honors placement is as follows: 75 (verbal skills), 75 (reading). Your daughter's scores are far below the minimum cut-off. Please also understand that we have a large number of students who score well above this bar. You mentioned that she received an A in Reading, but also that this interest just surfaced during eighth grade, which brings into question the level of preparedness.

Although I understand that you do not wish to witness her recent interest in literature wane, I would like to emphasize that our standard freshmen English classes are rigorous enough to challenge our students. She will be challenged in a Standard English class freshman year, where we would be able to fill in any gaps and afford her the opportunity to develop a solid foundation of not only critical reading, but also analytical writing. If she earns an A in standard college prep English freshman year, she will be moved into honors English sophomore year.

Kind regards,
Department Chair–English

First the good news: The department chair wrote a response that addressed most of the points that the parent brought up in the letter. Emma's parents asked for information about the process for requesting a specific class placement and the response back basically stated that no process existed for parents to make this request. Technically, the school response was a well-thought-out, well-written letter. However, those of you who are well on your way to adopting a growth mindset and read it through a growth mindset lens probably need to take a deep breath. I know I had to when I read this response. This kind of gatekeeping occurs through all grade levels in many schools. Emma is demonstrating enthusiasm, motivation, and willingness to welcome the challenge of an honors level course. The department chair is demonstrating a fixed mindset, a belief that this child does not have the innate ability to handle an honors level course based on a multicontent placement test given one morning of this child's life. If you analyze the response further, she also points out to the parents that the child fell "far below" their "cut-off." (Message to parents: "Your child is not smart.") If your class placement process even entertains the words "cut-off," then the process is not one that truly contributes to a growth mindset culture. Look at the response again and keep an eye out for other statements that scream, "We don't believe your child can do this!" The fact that the incoming student is referred to as a "candidate" also sends a message. Synonyms for "candidate" include contender, nominee, and contestant; the child simply wants to enroll in an honors class, not run for a political office. Also keep in mind that the decision to keep this child out of the course that she has the motivation to take was made without ever having met her. If the school or staff member was not willing to let the child into an honors-level course based on test scores, perhaps inviting the child in for an informal discussion about a book she has read and to gauge her motivation would have been an appropriate intermediate step that could have occurred. The way this situation played out is a clear example of gatekeeping and a fixed mindset mentality.

Sharing the above communication or one like it with staff can actually be an effective way to initiate a deep discussion with your team or staff about beliefs and school policies. Some educators may see nothing wrong with the above decision. If this is the case, challenge them to view it again through the lens of a fixed or growth mindset. What message does this send to a child? If a student has the motivation, persistence, and willingness to put forth the effort, is she allowed opportunities to be engaged in higher level classes in your school or district? Monitoring how teachers interact with students and communicate growth mindset messages is only part of the process. Evaluating current instructional practices and policies within the school or district is also imperative.

So what happened to Emma when she was kept out of the honors level class? Well, sadly, Emma no longer has a great enthusiasm for literature. There are probably several reasons why this occurred; the first being that she was not with a peer group in her English class who shared her enthusiasm for literature. Interpretive discussions were scant, differentiation did not occur, and she began to believe that well, maybe English was not her thing after all. Another contributor was that solid classroom management did not exist, and instructional time was used to get students in line and ready to learn. Although she was with a first-year teacher who showed great potential, management was not yet a strength. Content that was part of the freshmen English class was "covered," but the instruction lacked depth. Writing was not explicitly taught based on student strengths or needs, and when the parent asked for clarity about writing instruction, she was told (by the same department chair) that students were expected to know how to write when they entered the school.

Suffice it to say that due to the school and/or educator's fixed mindset and gatekeeping practices, a child who was ready to embrace a challenge and be successful now believes that she cannot do so. If policy makers at Emma's school were educated and believed in neuroscience studies that demonstrate the plasticity of the brain and the value of motivation, perhaps Emma could have developed her love of literature and possibly, could have become the author of a future great American novel.

CHAPTER 3

WHY IS A DIFFERENTIATED, RESPONSIVE CLASSROOM IMPORTANT TO A GROWTH MINDSET CULTURE?

"My brain is getting smarter and smarter each day."—Grade 1 student

The mindset of a teacher contributes greatly to his or her responsiveness to the needs of students. If an educator views a child through a deficit lens, then that child will not be given opportunities to grow unless she is in a responsive classroom. Deficit thinking is a practice of making assumptions about a child's ability based on perceived deficits or because of race, low-income status, English language acquisition, or a variety of other factors. Educators who value differentiated instruction need to be very aware about the beliefs they hold deep within themselves regarding student intelligence. I would argue that it is not possible to plan and facilitate an effective, differentiated, responsive classroom if an educator does not really possess the belief that intelligence can develop. Differentiation is responsive instruction. Ask five teachers what "differentiation" means to them and you are likely to get five different responses. To put it simply, differentiation is the way a teacher responds to a student's needs.

differentiation

the way a teacher responds to a student's needs so that each student is challenged at the appropriate level

Let's make an assumption that you have a growth mindset and want to be responsive to the potential in all of your students. Do you know how to effectively differentiate/be responsive to the needs of your students? What instructional structures are in place to guarantee a responsive learning environment? That seems to be the predicament that many teachers face. Once again, we find many new teachers graduate with a teaching degree but have never had even one class or accessed professional development in differentiation or responsive teaching. The focus of this chapter delineates the necessary steps to have a responsive, differentiated classroom.

Preview and Preassess

The initial stage of differentiation involves preassessment or finding out what students know about a particular skill, concept, or topic before planning for instruction. Preassessment is the first step to creating a differentiated classroom.

In the past, preassessment has been used for years in one particular subject area. Any guesses? Spelling! Historically, students have been given a spelling pretest on Monday and a posttest on Friday. What instructional changes occurred due to the range of outcomes indicated from the spelling pretest? Well, in some classrooms, teachers provided students with different spelling words to learn that were perhaps taken from their own writing. In other classrooms, the "reward" for knowing the words on Monday was more words! So these wonderful spellers *got to do* 30 words instead of 20! (Not a good practice, by the way.) Other times, students just took the pretest and regardless of what level of mastery was demonstrated, the whole class did the same spelling activities for the week and all took the same test on Friday. As this predicament shows, differentiation and a responsive classroom is not just about administering a preassessment, it is about reacting and responding to the results.

preassessment

finding out what students know about a particular skill, concept, or topic before planning for instruction

Preview the Content

It is important to learn and respect what students already bring to the classroom. However, before jumping into developing your own or using a ready-made preassessment, an important precursor must take place. You must allow students the opportunity to first "preview" the content being assessed. I know what some of you are thinking: "If I do that, it will be too easy" or "That's cheating!" Not so. In fact, previewing provides an opportunity for students to activate background knowledge and previous learning prior to a preassessment so that the results will be a better reflection of what they understand. Imagine that you're getting ready to sit down and read a new book. About 5 or 10 minutes into the storyline, something is triggered in your mind and you begin to think that perhaps you have read this book before. It starts feeling familiar to you, but the title did not ring a bell. Or maybe, you pick up the book at the library or bookstore and read the blurb on the back cover, and after doing so, remember that you have read it. That blurb activated background knowledge for you; it triggered your memory and served as a preview to the book. It is then that you have an "Aha!" moment and better recall the content of the book.

Previewing should not be a long drawn-out lesson: 5 minutes or less is usually enough time to activate prior knowledge. A preview could be as simple as telling students, "Today I would like to see what you know about rounding numbers. Let me show you a few first." Then, proceed to do a few examples on the board. The word "rounding" on a preassessment may not be familiar or trigger any past learning, but after that quick warm-up, lots of students will remember and be ready to show what they know about rounding. Other ways to preview include questioning, watching a short video, interpreting a picture, and listening to a poem or short story with discussion. It can be anything that will trigger previous learning on a topic. What is interesting is that sometimes a preview is all that some students might need to learn a new skill or concept.

The impact of previewing before preassessment became very clear for one sixth-grade English teacher. She was preparing a preassessment on figurative language for two different sections of sixth-grade English. For one of her classes, she showed a 3-minute animated video that she found online. This video was shown prior to the preassessment and reviewed common devices used in figurative language: simile, metaphor, and personification. After viewing the video she then asked her class to complete a paper-and-pencil preassessment requiring students to identify those devices and then write examples of various types of figurative language. She gave both classes the same preassessment but only previewed the material with one section. The results showed a much higher level of understanding for the students who previewed the material first. In fact, almost half of the previewed class showed complete understanding based upon the preassessment! Only a few students in the class who took the preassessment cold showed understanding of the concept. It is possible that a few of the students learned about similes, metaphors, and personification during that 3-minute video, but for the majority of students, the preview helped to simply "wake up" the prior learning in their minds.

Developing Preassessments

The effective use of preassessment is essential to ensuring that students and teachers both work from a growth mindset, believing that effort is the most important attribute that determines success. Without the use of preassessment, some students do not develop a good work ethic due to the fact that they are "learning" content that they already understand. Even though formative assessments can be used to help determine differentiation during the course of an instructional sequence, preassessments allow for front-end differentiation. (Many teachers differentiate for high-ability students at the end of a unit.) Front-end differentiation allows teachers to plan for valuable enrichment and can also provide an opportunity for students to accelerate within the content topic at the beginning of a learning sequence. Preassessment respects a student's time and prior knowledge.

Deciding what kind of preassessment to use depends upon the content being assessed. Preassessments do not always have to be paper-and-pencil tests. For example, in the primary grades you might ask students to demonstrate their knowledge using concrete math manipulatives or by conducting a structured discussion capturing understanding with anecdotal records or from teacher's notes. If you want to assess their knowledge of measurement, then hand them a ruler and see what they can do. In trying to have students recognize the author's point of view, a teacher may meet with small groups and, through a guided discussion, note ideas related to understanding the concept. In both of these cases, teachers should keep observational records that capture evidence of student understanding at a range of levels from concrete to more abstract.

If a paper-and-pencil preassessment is chosen, then it is important to think through how to develop assessment tools to best capture the understanding of the skill, concept, and content. In *Differentiation and the Brain: How Neuroscience Supports the Learner-Friendly Classroom* (Sousa & Tomlinson, 2011), the importance of providing multiple means of representation and expression when developing a preassessment is emphasized. When appropriate, be sure to include both words and pictures in directions and read the directions out loud. Students should also be provided with opportunities to communicate their understanding in various ways. Don't squeeze too many skills or concepts into one preassessment. For example, each math topic or unit can have its own preassessment; it is not appropriate to preassess for an entire year or semester. Besides, how would you preview all of those concepts and skills?

Ideally, preassessments should be built into the curriculum so that teachers do not have to develop them with each new topic or unit and so they can be consistent across classrooms and schools. With the transition to the Common Core State Standards taking place in many states, this is an ideal time to make that happen. Regardless of who is creating the assessment, the following should be considered during the development of preassessments:

1. The preassessment must measure understanding only in the areas that are specifically being assessed. In other words, if a child's understanding of U.S. history or a student's knowledge of Shakespeare is being assessed, spelling, grammar, and punctuation should not count. Spelling, grammar, and punctuation have nothing to do with a student's understanding of history or Shakespeare. Only if you were specifically assessing spelling, grammar, or punctuation would you consider those errors.

2. A preassessment should include application of the skill, topic, or concept and at least one above-level, or accelerated, indicator. You may be surprised at how deep and how far the understanding is for some students.

3. When configuring a preassessment, use different formats, allowing students to demonstrate understanding from recognizing an example to producing an example. Formats should vary within the same assessment: multiple choice, creating examples, fill in the blank, open-ended questions, completing a graphic organizer, and/or mind mapping, to name a few. Avoid true/false and other formats where a 50-50 guess exists; for math concepts, assess the concept in two ways if possible.

4. Use effective questions. "What kind of candy bar is in the sky?" is an example of a question that was found on a preassessment that was developed to measure student understanding of the solar system. (The teacher was going for "Milky Way," but "Mars" would also work.) The issue with this question is that it does not really give the teacher information. I might know that the Milky Way is in the sky but have no knowledge of what it is. A better way to measure understanding might be the following: "The Milky Way is a galaxy that contains our solar system. Share everything that you know about the Milky Way."

5. If reading is not being assessed, read the preassessment to the students. Reading the preassessment levels the playing field for those students who are not yet strong readers. They will be able to demonstrate understanding of the content without worrying about misinterpreting directions or not knowing a word or phrase.

Guidelines for developing a preassessment specific to math can be found in Figure 2. Even though these guidelines are directed toward math preassessments, they can be applied to other subject areas as well. Teachers should avoid preassessing and teaching the same topics, skills, procedures, or concepts on the same day. Educators need time to analyze the results and plan for instruction. It is also important to note that preassessments should never count toward a child's grade and that it is important to frame the purpose of the task with the students. Let students know that the information they share will help determine how to approach instruction for them. It is important that they put forth their best effort but that they realize the grade will not count on their report card. One first-grade teacher reported that some of her students cried when completing a preassessment because she did not frame the task properly; they felt frustrated and worried about their lack of knowledge.

When beginning to evaluate student preassessments, another important consideration is how you analyze the outcome. It is not an all-or-nothing approach and assigning a random percentage is not

Guidelines for Developing Preassessments for Math

1. The preassessment must measure understanding only in the topic/unit that is specifically being assessed and include both computation/procedural skills and a measurement of conceptual understanding.
2. Make it clear in the teacher resources that teachers should read the preassessment directions out loud so all students understand what is being asked. (A struggling reader should not be penalized in math because he or she cannot read the directions.)
3. Include a few sentences for teachers to read to students prior to the preassessment. This should help frame the reason for the preassessment (i.e., "Today I want to see what you know about fractions. This task will not count as a grade but it is very important for you to do your best. This will help me plan instruction that is just right for you.").
4. Go deep. A math preassessment is not just about computation. A preassessment should include application of the mathematical skill or concept.
5. When possible, a math preassessment should ask students to reason quantitatively with the concept.
6. When developing a preassessment, use different formats, allowing students to demonstrate understanding from solving a problem to developing a problem. Avoid true/false, multiple choice, and other formats where a students can guess an answer.
7. Assess each math skill or concept in at least two ways.
8. Include above-grade-level indicators within the same topic.

Figure 2. Guidelines for developing a preassessment specific to math.

responsive to specific student needs. Therefore, saying that all students who get an 85% or greater are ready to move on is not appropriate or responsive to students. That randomly assigned number of 85 tells us nothing about where the specific student's strengths and needs lie. The purpose is to find students who have partial or complete understanding, then figure out where the gaps are and how to plan instructionally for those students. When students show partial understanding, note the areas that need to be addressed. It is helpful to develop a matrix that lists all of the objectives that were assessed and all of the students' names. Teachers can then color code, use a check system, or assign points to each of the objectives. These will help form flexible groups and the instructional planning that takes place will consider the needs of the students before instruction even begins. Even better, if preassessments are developed centrally in a school system, an electronic tool can be developed that would capture student performance on a preassessment or allow for teachers to input data and make recommendations as to the areas that need to be revisited, where content gaps can be filled in, and most importantly, what instruction can be eliminated—in other words, where to compact the curriculum.

Curriculum Compacting

Curriculum compacting was originally developed by Joseph Renzulli and Linda Smith many, many years ago. It is interesting that it is a relatively "old" strategy that few teachers know about. When preparing to teach graduate school courses on the topic of differentiation, I always send out an electronic preassessment to try to gauge the understanding of the students prior to the start of the course. The results help me adjust the pacing based on the needs of the class as a whole (not to mention that differentiation is being modeled for the students). Without fail, every time I analyze the results, the area that surfaces as the greatest need for my students is curriculum compacting. Most don't even know what it is, and the graduate students who know what it is do not know how to implement it.

Curriculum compacting is an instructional strategy that streamlines grade-level curriculum by eliminating content that students have previously learned. Think about what a trash compactor does: It takes a large amount of trash and compacts it down to a little bit of space. Now think about curriculum (I am by no means referring to curriculum as trash!): For some students, that big expanse of curriculum can be taught in less time, and some of this curriculum can even be eliminated for some students. Compacting buys time for students to go deeper and wider into the content and/or accelerate to above-grade-level indicators. Does every child in your class need

39

the same amount of time to read and discuss a novel? Understand and apply a mathematical process? Educators must be willing to compact curriculum for those students who are ready to go on. How do we know when they are ready?

curriculum compacting

an instructional strategy that streamlines grade-level curriculum by eliminating content that students have previously learned

The preassessment plays a major role in determining candidates for curriculum compacting. Other behaviors in the classroom also give us clues. For example, if a student shows great interest and motivation in a particular area of study, then we know we can move him or her into deeper understanding of those concepts. For example, Mr. Smith previewed and preassessed student knowledge of World War II and several students demonstrated a strong conceptual understanding of this time in history. However, Mr. Smith was not really sure about one student, Patrick. Even though Patrick's preassessment results clearly showed some background knowledge of the topic, it was not enough to decide if Patrick needed compacting. Mr. Smith decided to take a few minutes before class to discuss World War II with this student. After only a few minutes, he clearly saw an enthusiastic interest in the topic from Patrick. The student demonstrated a thirst for knowledge in the subject and asked Mr. Smith great questions. This exchange, in combination with the preassessment, gave Mr. Smith the data he needed to determine that Patrick needed to be in the compacting group for this unit of study.

Other behaviors that suggest a need for compacting include students who consistently finish work early and accurately and those who express an interest in pursuing advanced topics. Another clue to the need for compacting can surface in those students who often create their own diversions in class. Many of the students who create these distractions do so because they have time to. In other words, they have finished their work and are filling their time with less productive behaviors.

Renzulli, Smith, and Reis (1982) developed a tool to assist teachers in planning for compacting. Their Compactor tool provides teachers with an opportunity to define the outcomes of instruction, then determine and document the students who have complete or partial mastery and provide replacement options for those students who need it. The Compactor can serve as a useful conceptual tool for teachers when they begin to implement compacting in their classroom, with one exception—the third column of the compactor is entitled "Acceleration and/or Enrichment Activities." Educators need to be careful when interpreting the word "activities," as this alternate opportunity is about instruction, not just an activity. What alternative *instruction* will these students receive as a result of compacting? Too often students are just given worksheets or an extra "activity" to complete as a way to "differentiate" for them. Instruction at their readiness level is what they need, not a worksheet, independent activity, or more of the same.

Flexible Grouping

Preassessment and compacting are necessary components when creating flexible small groups in the classroom. Teachers may find that, after preassessment, no students need compacting, that all of the students show enough understanding that they would benefit from taking less time and eliminating material. Also consider that some students have such a deep understanding of a topic that they have no gaps to fill. They don't need compacting; they simply need to move on. Although the Common Core State Standards go deeper into learning, it is still important to consider adding a thin layer of enrichment for students who demonstrate mastery before they are accelerated to above-level content. This enrichment will make sure that students are not prematurely moving on. A thin layer means just that: a small amount of enrichment. Spending days on end revisiting and enriching mastered material in new ways does

41

not provide appropriate challenge and is not respectful of the student's prior knowledge.

Maintaining flexible small groups across content areas is an essential component of a differentiated, growth mindset class culture. Traditionally, elementary classrooms incorporate flexible groups in reading only. Perhaps movement among these groups is not as fluid as it should be, but most primary classrooms operate several reading groups. Why does this occur only in reading and often only in primary grades? Students have varied levels in math as well, yet many classrooms deliver whole-group math instruction. Once students begin middle and high school, an assumption is made that they are "grouped" already. Perhaps a school offers honors or remedial sections in reading or math. Often an assumption is made that subgrouping within a classroom should not occur because of the availability of leveled classes. The fact is that a large range exists within these classes and differentiation with flexible grouping should be an important tenet of classes that are already homogeneously grouped. Let's go back to the belief that kids can get smarter. If all students in a classroom are instructed at the same level, what opportunities exist to challenge those students who are ready to embrace a more rigorous learning experience? The bottom line is that if we walk into any classroom, in any content area, at any grade level, evidence of flexible grouping should exist. It may not be an everyday occurrence at the secondary level, but it should be an important component of the class structure and used routinely. Teachers often share reasons why flexible grouping does not occur, and the reason that surfaces most often is management. How can we effectively manage multiple groupings in the classroom?

Management

Clear expectations are the single most important aspect of managing multiple groups in the classroom. What are students supposed to do when they are done with their work? What should they do if they need help and you are working with another group of students? Spending time modeling and communicating expectations for independent work time is time well spent. If, for example, three instructional groups exist in a class, then instructional time should occur with each group during the time block. During a 90-minute reading/language arts block in the elementary classroom, the teacher might spend 25 minutes with each group and allow for time between groups to touch base with students to answer any questions and to make sure everyone is on the right track. At the secondary level, a teacher might use a 45-minute period to meet with two groups for 20 minutes each. So what should students be working on while the teacher is facilitating another group? The other groups should be working on meaningful tasks that will complement the content area they are working on. This might be independent study or could also be a group task.

Carol Ann Tomlinson, who has authored many books on differentiation, suggested incorporating anchor activities into classrooms in her 2001 book, *How to Differentiate Instruction in Mixed-Ability Classrooms*. Anchor activities are ongoing tasks that students work on independently when they complete classroom work or when their teacher is working with other students. Anchors should enrich the learning of the content being studied. They are similar to centers but are typically available for the duration of a unit of study, quarter, or semester. For example, if students were learning about the election process in the United States, the anchor activities would also be about the election process. Or if you were implementing the professional development plan on mindsets and intelligence discussed in Chapter 1, you might provide the following anchor activity to the teachers/staff members:

> If you finish an activity or reading early, please look through this folder and choose an article of interest that discusses various aspects of persistence, motivation, effort, and malleable intelligence.

Anchors can also serve as an opportunity to enrich learning by going deeper into the subject area. These tasks extend the learning and are developed as tasks that can be completed successfully independent of the teacher. Anchor activities are not busy work! They are meaningful tasks that are a natural extension of student learning. Take, for example, a class studying the U.S. election process, the teacher might be extending the learning of a group of students who demonstrated understanding based on a preassessment. The rest of the class is reading and answering some questions about what they read. Two of these students finish their work so they now have an opportunity to visit some anchor activities. In this case, the teacher has developed an anchor requiring the analysis of political cartoons. The students find a file of political cartoons from U.S. history that communicate a message about political parties or a special historical election. Using guiding questions and/or a graphic organizer, students analyze the message of the cartoon. They may even categorize cartoons together that send a similar message. This task is meaningful and requires critical thinking while freeing the teacher up to work with another group of students. An added bonus is that this type of anchor does not require a grade, because it is interpretive. The students simply need to put forth effort and justify their thinking.

anchor activities

ongoing tasks given to students that they can access when they complete classroom work or when their teacher is working with other students and that enrich the learning of the content being studied

Many resources are available online for developing anchor activities; check the Resources section of this book for a recommended site. You may even want to develop some anchors that have to do with the malleability of the brain! It is well worth the time investment, as it will make managing differentiated groups a breeze.

Acceleration and Enrichment

Which is more important: acceleration or enrichment? OK, trick question—they are equally important. Think about enrichment as going deep and wide into the content and acceleration as going forward. Acceleration can take many forms and is not just about grade skipping. It is about allowing students who have already mastered content as evidenced by a preassessment coupled with observation of students who master content quickly to move on. Every student deserves to learn every day. Preassessment and curriculum compacting allow for topic/content area acceleration. A growth mindset on the part of both the teacher and the student is necessary for acceleration. Too many times I have heard teachers say, "He would not be able to handle acceleration," "She gets off task easily so I will not accelerate," or "He is on a behavior contract." These "excuses" or attempts to rationalize gatekeeping are not part of a responsive classroom. Topic or content area acceleration is not a reward; it is a necessity for those students who have demonstrated mastery and are ready to embrace more challenge.

acceleration

moving faster through content, allowing students who have already mastered content or who master content quickly to move into above-grade-level content

Enrichment is about going deeper into the learning. Can students apply the skill, concept, or process to different situations? Can they think critically about the content? Do students have the ability to reason with the material? It is usually a good idea to add at least a thin layer of enrichment before acceleration, especially if the preassessment captures only a surface level of understanding. If the preassessment measures the depth of understanding—for example, application of the concept or skill—then perhaps the student is ready to be accelerated without making an enrichment stop.

Whether acceleration and/or enrichment occur, it is important to look carefully at instructional experiences to make sure they are laden with opportunities to think critically.

enrichment

learning with greater depth and breadth; going deep and wide into the content

Formative Assessment

Formative assessment, or checking for understanding, is nonnegotiable in a responsive, growth mindset classroom. Checking for understanding during the course of instruction contributes to opportunities for students to have access to complex and engaging instruction. It is through formative assessment that educators determine the content and the pace by which students grasp concepts. Through formative assessment, teachers also learn who has not yet grasped a concept and make plans to approach the instruction again in a new way. Ongoing, formative assessment plays a crucial role in teacher decision making and should be routinely used across all content areas.

Douglas Fisher and Nancy Frey, authors of *Checking for Understanding: Formative Assessment Techniques for Your Classroom* (2007) described formative assessment well:

> Formative assessments are ongoing assessments, reviews, and observations in a classroom. Teachers use formative assessment to improve instructional methods and provide student feedback throughout the teaching and learning process. For example, if a teacher observes that some students do not grasp a concept, he or she can design a review activity to reinforce the concept or use a different instructional strategy to reteach it. (p. 4)

formative assessment

checking for understanding during the learning process in order to modify instruction to improve understanding; this is an assessment *for* learning

Formative assessment is a reflective tool for a teacher. It should not be graded. It is a quick check to help the teacher become informed of where students are on the path to learning. Formative assessments help teachers find out who needs to be retaught, who is on track, and who needs enrichment and acceleration. If the majority of students do not have success, then teachers should do as Fisher and Frey (2007) noted: reflect on the way the material was taught, come up with a new way to present the material, and reteach it.

Formative assessment is also a checkpoint for student understanding. Teachers can use the data from formative assessments to keep groups fluid and flexible. If a child starts out in an on-level group and comprehends the material at a faster pace than his peer group, then the teacher should move the child to a group that will challenge him. Through ongoing assessment, students will be provided with more opportunities to access enriched learning opportunities.

Formative assessment does not have to be complicated. Keep it simple. The following are a few ideas for implementing formative assessment in your classroom:

- *Use questions for students to respond to orally.* During the course of instruction or on the way out of the door (in middle school and high school), ask students to respond to various questions regarding the learning that occurred during class. Make note of those students who have misunderstandings or have not yet grasped the learning. (This method can also help some students focus their attention during the learning if they know they will be asked about it during or after class.)

- *Use questions for students to respond to in writing.* Provide students with a few questions that will help them communicate their understanding of a concept.
- *Use exit cards.* Provide a prompt on an exit card that each student fills out at the end of an instructional experience. It might be a math problem, a sentence that needs grammar corrections, a question about why or how an historical event came to be, or a statement asking for a summary of the content learned.
- *Use a 3-2-1.* A 3-2-1 can be customized depending on the content and grade level. A generic form of a 3-2-1 might provide students an opportunity to express orally or in writing the following: 3 Things I Learned Today, 2 Things I Have Questions About, 1 Thing That I Want to Learn More About. See Figure 3 for an example of a 3-2-1.
- *Listen to and observe students.* Observing students during a science lab, working a math problem, or completing an in-class writing assignment or listening to them discussing a novel can also serve as a formative assessment.

Without formative assessment, the following scenario is bound to happen frequently: A science teacher introduces a new concept to a class of students. He lectures for about 40 minutes using a PowerPoint presentation and explaining the concept. For homework, each student is given a worksheet to complete based on the information he taught that day. Students do the homework and turn it in. After checking their grades online, many find that they received an "F" for their homework.

Now, let's think about this for a minute. The homework could have served as a formative assessment had the teacher approached it differently. After glancing at the homework at the beginning of class, he could have seen that many of the students did not have an understanding of the concept. At that point, he could have used time to go over the homework, clarify, and reteach if necessary. If anchor activities were in place in the class, then the few students who showed mastery might be given the choice to do them or to

	Formative Assessment About the Brain	
	Name _____ Date _____	
3	Things I learned:	
2	Things I have a question about:	
1	Thing about the brain that I want to learn more about:	

Figure 3. Example of a 3-2-1 formative assessment.

participate in the clarification/reteaching session. The other red flag is that the students did not get the papers back to see where the errors were, they simply saw a grade online. The teacher was holding off giving back the papers until an absent student had the chance to turn his in. Homework can be used as a formative assessment (as long as you are sure it is the student's work) and should never receive a letter grade. Grades for homework should indicate completion, not accuracy, especially when students are still on the pathway to understanding.

When implementing formative assessment, let students know why you assess formatively and that it helps you as a teacher adjust and better meet their needs. Let them know that you always want to improve and grow as a teacher. This models a teacher's own growth mindset for his or her students. Formative assessment improves teaching and learning, and it allows for growth in all students.

Summative Assessment

You have previewed, preassessed, compacted the curriculum for some learners, formed instructional groups, and provided opportunities for enriched learning and accelerated content. Whew! Well done. Now it is time to think about how you will assess understanding or mastery of the content. Giving the same summative assessment (assessment *of* the learning), performance task, or product assignment is not an option when working with different instructional groups. The assessment must match the learning that has taken place for each group or, in some cases, an individual student. If students will be demonstrating understanding through a product, then make sure choices are offered. Grades should be based on mastery of the content that was tailored to the student. If grades were given solely on mastery of on-grade-level curriculum, then students could potentially earn an A after the preassessment, before any instruction even occurred. In this scenario, a child has put forth no effort and yet is rewarded with an A. It is this kind of situation that contributes to the development of a fixed mindset. Students begin to feel that they must always look smart, that putting forth effort shows weakness, and that they are expected to know things without trying After all, their whole lives they have been told they are "smart," and if you are smart, everything should come easy, right? Wrong. Students must be challenged appropriately. Be sure that your assessments, both formative and summative, are differentiated for each group.

summative assessment

assessment *of* learning that typically occurs at the end of a unit of study

A Final Thought About Differentiated, Responsive Instruction

As mentioned previously, the process described above is what I refer to as front-end differentiated, responsive instruction. It is about respecting and responding to what a child needs when she walks in the door and as she makes her way through the learning. Too often, differentiation occurs on the back end of instruction. The teacher figures out at the end of a unit or learning sequence that a student needs more. The "more" is too often interpreted as more of the same or more papers or "activities" rather than more responsive instruction. Provide opportunities for students to be challenged from the beginning. Be responsive to their needs and the potential of all they can accomplish.

Template for Planning

In Figures 4 and 5, you will find a template that helps visualize the differentiation/responsive teaching process and a checklist for you to use as you begin the process.

The template in Figure 4 is a way to reflect on, think about, and set up the instruction; it does not include specific instructional strategies. However, care should be taken to differentiate process or strategies among the groups. Differentiation of process is about how the learning is presented and how a student interacts with the material. Also note that the differentiation model described is focused on readiness, not student interest; student interest should be considered when planning any instructional sequence. Many teachers find this template helpful for planning for differentiation. Once educators internalize the process, this planning shell may not be needed. Several teachers use the template to record the names of the students in each group on the back of each column or replicate the template electronically and record student data; this can serve as way to keep track of where students begin and how far they go in a specific unit, topic, or concept.

Eric Jensen, author of 2005's *Teaching With the Brain in Mind*, pointed out that "Research on brain maturation clearly indicates that the commonly mandated policy of 'everyone on the same page on the same day' makes little sense" (p. 151), a statement that lends support to both differentiation and grouping in growth mindset cultures. Keeping the possibility of three instructional groups (at the elementary level; you can use two instructional groups at the secondary level) in mind, as illustrated on this template, complements the building of a growth mindset culture. With practice, effort, motivation, and, yes, a growth mindset, differentiated, responsive instruction can become the heart of instruction. Responding to the needs of all learners is a responsibility that we all have as educators.

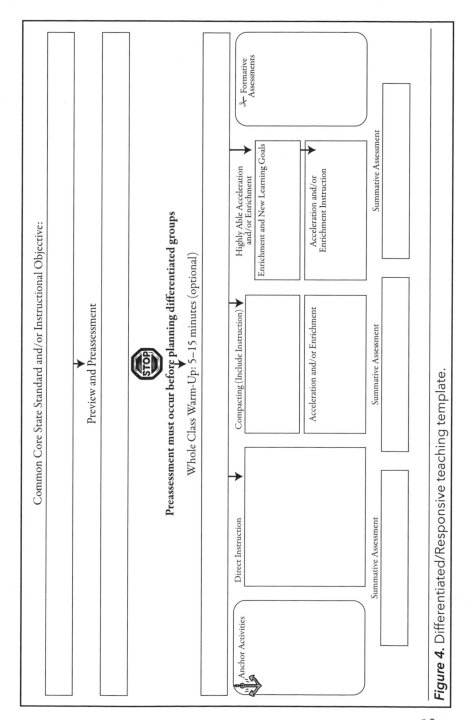

Figure 4. Differentiated/Responsive teaching template.

Teacher Checklist for Planning
Differentiated, Responsive Instruction

❑ Determine skills, content, concepts, or procedures being assessed and develop or use school/district preassessment.

❑ Develop anchor activities related to the unit.

❑ Present preview (2–5 minutes) to activate background knowledge prior to preassessment.

❑ Students take preassessment.

❑ Analyze preassessments: determine areas already mastered, any gaps that may exist, and areas of need for each student.

❑ Identify students who would benefit from curriculum compacting and plan instruction for the areas of need.

❑ Identify any students who have complete understanding and are ready for another learning outcome. Plan for enrichment and topic/content acceleration for these students.

❑ Form instructional groups—model anchor activity expectations if necessary and share the group rotation for the day. Teacher will instruct each group every day. Plan for a few minutes between groups to respond to any questions from students, make sure everyone is on the right track, and praise effort students are putting forth.

❑ Administer formative assessment daily. Use the information to inform instruction for students as well reflection for the teacher. If understanding is not evident with most students, reteach in a new way. Student movement among groups may occur based on the formative assessments.

❑ Summative assessments, performance tasks, and products (as well as homework) must be differentiated based on the instruction for each group.

Figure 5. Differentiation checklist.

CHAPTER 4

WHY IS CRITICAL THINKING IMPORTANT IN A GROWTH MINDSET CLASS CULTURE?

> "I don't mind if I mess up an assignment, as long as I figure out what I did wrong."
> —Grade 6 student

What is the relationship between critical thinking and growth mindset? Let's first take a moment and agree on a definition of critical thinking. Daniel Willingham (2008), professor of cognitive psychology at the University of Virginia, gave solid research on the development of critical thinking in our schools. Willingham shared that, from a cognitive scientist's point of view, three types of thinking fall under the umbrella of critical thinking: reasoning, making judgments/decisions, and problem solving. Every day we reason, problem solve, and make decisions, but they do not always require critical thought. For example, when you woke up this morning one of the first decisions that you had to make was what to wear. Is this a decision that required critical thought? In most cases, no; however, is there ever a time when deciding what to wear does require critical thought? Perhaps if you were planning a day of hiking in a terrain where temperatures can change dramatically or you had an important job interview; in these cases, deciding what to wear could require a small amount of critical thought. Students may be given opportunities to reason, make decisions, or problem solve, but the question we must ask ourselves as educators is if these opportunities require deep, critical thinking.

Another important factor to consider about critical thinking is that it is not a simple skill (Willingham, 2008). According to Willingham (2008), critical thinking is a process that must be infused with content; it is not something that you can just check off a list once it is mastered. Why? Well, one reason is that the content being focused on and the complexity of thinking critically becomes more sophisticated over time—it is always evolving. The practice component applied to the content knowledge is essential to develop learners who can apply critical thinking when they need to. Hand in hand with practice is persistence and effort, probably the two most important attributes of having a growth mindset!

If you embrace Willingham's argument that critical thinking is not a bunch of isolated skills, then you too (like me) may become annoyed by the amount of resources on the market that advertise ways to build critical thinking "skills." Due in part to the way critical thinking is framed in these resources, the concept of accepting critical thinking as a process embedded in content rather than a set of skills can require a major shift in thinking.

Critical Thinking in School

During a professional development workshop, one teacher disagreed with the idea that critical thinking is not a skill. In the process of her argument, she explained that cooking is a skill that can never be mastered because the complexity grows, just like thinking critically. I knew where she was coming from—she made the assumption that cooking itself was a skill. Not so—it is a process that requires many skills. She was correct in her analogy that cooking can become more complex just like critical thinking, and she provided me with an opportunity to expand her analogy. Cooking is not a skill but a process, a process that requires certain skills: measurement skills, knife skills, following directions, reading skills, etc. Critical thinking is a process that also requires skills. The skills required vary depending on the situation. For example, if a student is required to analyze data, he may need to use classification skills. The skill of classifying can be taught, practiced, and applied to a variety of situations from an early age. We want to start thinking about critical thinking as a process of strategies that can be applied to myriad situations rather than a set of skills.

Often, expectations are low for students who do not show strength in the traditional areas of schooling: reading, writing, and math. When students are viewed through a lens of achievement (or intelligence in some cases), opportunities for critical thinking are fewer for those students who are on the perceived lower end. It usually boils down to what reading or math level they are functioning on. Students who are from culturally, linguistically, and/or ethnically diverse populations, special education students, and yes, even sometimes those students who demonstrate challenging behaviors are often not provided with rigorous instructional opportunities. These students would benefit tremendously from ongoing, critical thinking experiences, yet these are the students who typically get the fewest critical thinking opportunities thanks to a fixed mindset from the point of view of the adult or the students themselves. By providing students with many opportunities to develop their cognitive abilities through critical thinking experiences, it impacts the child's view of herself and contributes to a growth mindset.

The Critical Thinking Growth Mindset Project

I was anxious to test my theory about how cognitive abilities can be changed through critical thinking experiences in schools with high poverty and lower achievement and developed a program that would put it to the test. Thus, the Critical Thinking Growth Mindset Project was born. This project involved six Title I schools, a total of 53 grade 2 and grade 3 classrooms. All grade 2 and grade 3 teachers, as well as some English for Speakers of Other Languages (ESOL) teachers in these Title I schools attended ongoing professional development that focused on building a growth mindset culture in their classroom. The professional development also included critical thinking professional development sessions. Part of the critical thinking professional learning sessions highlighted places where critical thinking processes were already embedded in their curriculum. Consideration of the critical thinking that is embedded in the Common Core State Standards for Mathematical Practice was also highlighted. Several of these eight mathematical practices complemented the goals of the project, with practice #1 and # 2 being the most emphasized.

- Practice #1: Make sense of problems and persevere in solving them.
- Practice #2: Reason abstractly and quantitatively.
- Practice #3: Construct viable arguments and critique the reasoning of others.
- Practice #5: Use appropriate tools strategically.

Professional development for the first year of the project focused on ways that teachers could build students' reasoning abilities, therefore the teachers learned instructional strategies that develop reasoning across all content areas. These included strategies that focused on deductive, analogical, and quantitative reasoning, as well as concept attainment and concept formation strategies. (Note that several of these strategies are embedded in the student lessons that were provided for the teachers. See Chapter 8 for examples of these lessons.)

Nonverbal Reasoning Games and Their Outcomes on Mindset in the Critical Thinking Growth Mindset Project

Embedding opportunities to reason in different ways with a variety of materials as often as possible was a goal for these classrooms. It was decided that another layer would be added by introducing some engaging nonverbal reasoning games into the classrooms. But first, it would be important to allow teachers to interact with these games so that they could really understand the challenge that students would face while progressing through the levels of the games. After review of many games, it was decided that each of the 53 classrooms would receive five specially selected games from Thinkfun, a company that specializes in developing games that build reasoning skills. The games that were chosen, ShapeOmetry (formerly known as TopThis!), Chocolate Fix, Brick by Brick, Rush Hour, and Math Dice Jr, specifically practiced quantitative and deductive reasoning in a nonverbal format. The games also increased the level of challenge as the children made their way up through each level. The project now had three important components:

1. Teachers and students building a growth mindset culture, including development of a conceptual understanding of basic brain function.
2. Teachers using instructional strategies that nurtured and developed critical thinking processes, specifically reasoning.
3. Access to nonverbal reasoning games that would be used as math anchor activities or warm-ups and would be available during inside recess, before and after school, etc.

All teachers were asked to record any instruction that focused on building a growth mindset culture, teaching students about the brain, and critical thinking using an electronic implementation tracker. Students were responsible for keeping track of the games they played and the levels they attained using an individual game tracker.

As a result of adding the specifically chosen reasoning games to the project, an outcome surfaced that was unexpected. The addition of the games did something more than build the reasoning abilities of these students; the reasoning and problem solving games contributed to a mindset shift in the teachers and, in some cases, the students as well. Many teachers reported that they saw potential in students that they would have never seen without the games. Some of the students who spoke little English flourished when the games came out. Some students who were functioning below grade level showed great strength in reasoning through playing these games. Teachers became more reflective about their own mindsets, viewed students differently, and raised expectations for many students. The games became an unexpected vehicle for building growth mindsets in the teachers and the students. As Holly, one of the third-grade ESOL teachers, reported:

> I first taught the game to my struggling ESOL students, giving them plenty of time to become familiar with the game and to formulate strategies for problem solving. Once they were comfortable and conversant about their strategies, I sent them out into the classroom to "teach" the rest of the class how to play. This was a powerful tool for their language development, as well as their self-esteem. These games contributed greatly to the growth mindset culture being developed in the class.

The games, in partnership with growth mindset lessons, also appeared to increase motivation for students. About 4 weeks into the project, I was visiting a classroom to demonstrate how neurons connected every time the students learned something new. After the lesson, the teacher was going right into math instructional time and had partnered students together to work with the games while she worked with a small group of students at her table. I decided to walk around this second-grade classroom and ask the students some questions as they played their reasoning games. With their permission, I used my phone to record these conversations. Here is an example of one of those conversations with two ESOL boys as they played Thinkfun's ShapeOmetry:

> *Mrs. Ricci:* So what's going on in your brain when you are playing this game?
> *Students*: We are making connections.
> *Mrs. Ricci:* What kinds of connections?
> *Students*: Connections like those . . . what are the names of those? numerals?
> *Mrs. Ricci:* Neurons?
> *Students*: Yes, those neurons are sticking together in my head.
> *Mrs. Ricci:* Do you ever feel like giving up?
> *Students*: No, never.
> *Mrs. Ricci*: Why?
> *Students*: It is easy
> *Mrs. Ricci:* Was it always easy?
> *Students*: No, not always easy,
> *Mrs. Ricci:* Why is it easier now?
> *Students*: We just, well we did it for about 5 days and it got easier because we practiced.
> *Mrs. Ricci:* Oh, so you practiced? So the more you practiced then what happened?
> *Students*: We made more connections in our brains and it gets easier!

You can see from that short conversation that these students are visualizing neural connections as they learn. Even though the child said "numerals" instead of "neurons" and said they were "sticking together in my head" rather than "making connections in my brain," he still had a solid conceptual understanding of what was happening and that understanding increased his perseverance and motivation to get through the tougher levels of the game. This can then be transferred to situations where a child might be struggling. For example, a teacher might say:

> Do you remember when you first played ShapeOmetry and it was hard? You practiced and persevered and made strong connections in your brain. Is it still just as hard for you? Now let's look at this math the same way. It might feel very challenging at first but with practice and perseverance you are making more connections in your brain and getting smarter!

Referring back to the process the students went through using the reasoning game helped get the conversation going about staying motivated when faced with challenging tasks. In some cases, students asked for "harder stuff" to help their brain grow.

The following is another example of a dialogue with two ESOL grade 2 students playing Rush Hour. The students began by explaining to me how to play the game. Then the conversation continued with one of the students:

> *Mrs. Ricci:* Do you ever feel like giving up?
> *Student:* No!
> *Mrs. Ricci:* Why?
> *Student:* I would give up playing a game like . . . Hide and Go Seek, but not this game.
> *Mrs. Ricci:* Why wouldn't you give up playing this game?
> *Student:* I am not giving up!
> *Mrs. Ricci:* Tell me why.
> *Student:* Well, first I think it is above grade level, and I think I can really do this thing!
> *Mrs. Ricci:* What makes you think that you can do it?
> *Student:* Because when I try, I know I am getting smarter by making connections and the new connections will help me do it!

62

This dialogue is such a wonderful example of student perseverance. The reference he made to "above grade level" made it clear that in his mind he was tackling a very challenging task. What a great example of a student welcoming challenge! He was determined to have success. His reference to Hide and Go Seek was interesting. Perhaps he does not view Hide and Go Seek as strategic or challenging, therefore he would give up because it would not be giving his brain a workout. In all eight informal interviews that were conducted with these groups of students, not one student said that he or she ever felt like giving up. As one of the ESOL students put it, "The more you try, the more you get smarter." Many teachers reported that they felt the games coupled with the growth mindset discussions increased perseverance. I suspect that if the games were just placed in the classrooms without the benefits of the growth mindset lessons and discussions, these conversations would have played out differently. My hunch is that many of these students would have given up in an early level of the game.

Results of the Critical Thinking Growth Mindset Project

The Critical Thinking Growth Mindset Project showed unexpected results in just 7 months. Not only did the teachers report increased motivation and persistence, but the data showed growth in reasoning for the students in these schools. Part of the school district's process for gifted and talented screening was the use of a cognitive abilities test. Scores from Title I schools were consistently well below the target score. In order to be considered for accelerated and/or enriched instruction, as well as identified as "gifted," this system used multiple criteria. One criterion was a target score of the 80th percentile on analogical and quantitative reasoning subtests. In the spring of their second-grade year, students across the district participated in a process for gifted services and identification. The mean scores for the six schools is shown in Table 2.

You can see how depressed these scores were. After just 7 months into the project, scores improved dramatically (see Table 3).

Table 2
Mean Scores for Students Before the Critical Thinking Growth Mindset Project

	Analogical Reasoning Percentile Mean Score	Quantitative Reasoning Percentile Mean Score	Target Percentile
2011	51	43	80
2010	50	43	80

Table 3
Scores of Students After 7 Months in the Critical Thinking Growth Mindset Project

	Analogical Reasoning Percentile Mean Score	Quantitative Reasoning Percentile Mean Score	Target Percentile
2012	59 (+8)	50 (+7)	80
2011	51	43	80
2010	50	43	80

All six schools averaged growth of 8 percentile points in analogical reasoning and 7 percentile points for quantitative reasoning.

One school made a jump of 21 percentile points on the quantitative reasoning subtest and another jumped 14 points in analogical reasoning. Although there is still a long way to go to get close to the benchmark, realize that we were on to something. That "something" is the combination of a growth mindset partnered with increased opportunities for critical thinking. Take a look at the following comments made by some of the teachers at the end of the first year of the project:

- "The perspective of students shifted completely. Whenever there was a difficult task, students would talk about determination, motivation, and persistence."

- "I found that their beliefs about how they can 'grow smart' changed as they would encourage each other by saying things like, 'You can do it!' and 'You can get smarter if you try harder!'"
- "My students constantly referred to having growth mindsets when setbacks occurred; it was great!"
- "I noticed a huge difference in student critical thinking as well as students' core beliefs that they could try hard and keep trying and succeed. I heard much less 'I can't' and more 'I have to keep trying.'"
- "Thinking and working hard became a 'mindset' in my classroom. We all worked together, learned from our mistakes, and challenged our brains to grow. The students have become really good at believing in themselves."

Critical thinking and a growth mindset culture go hand in hand. We can expect students to embrace challenge only if we make it available to them on a consistent basis.

CHAPTER 5

HOW CAN STUDENTS LEARN FROM FAILURE?

> "Failure is necessary for success. The more we try to avoid it, the less successful we are. Failure should be embraced, not avoided"—Garrett, Grade 12 student

As a parent, it is always difficult to see one of my children fail, especially if much effort was put into accomplishing the task. Think about the child who dedicates herself to studying for a test, working on a paper, or practicing a skill and then the reward is failure. Reward? Yes, failure can be a reward, for it is through failure that we can learn the most. There is a wonderful scene in Disney's *Meet the Robinsons* movie where Lewis creates an invention that combines peanut butter and jelly and it fails. As he buries his face in his hands and apologizes, the adults happily yell, "You've failed! From failure, you learn, from success . . . not so much."

Responding to Failure

The way we respond to failures and mistakes depends on our mindset. When we truly believe that intelligence is malleable, it is then that we realize that when we make a mistake—when we fail—we need to approach the task differently and/or put more effort into it. On the other hand, those who hold a fixed view of intelligence typically do not attempt to learn from their errors. Jason S. Moser of Michigan State University (who collaborated on his study with Hans S. Schroder, Carrie Heeter, Tim P. Moran, and Yu-Hao Lee) wanted some insight as to how people react to failure. These researchers gave participants a task that was purposefully designed for them to experience an error. Study subjects were asked to name the middle letter of a five-letter series. Sometimes the middle letter was the same as all of the other letters like, MMMMM; other times the middle letter was different, MMNMM. Even though the task sounds simple, once this is repeated several times, the brain can get sluggish, which is when people can begin to make mistakes.

Participants in the study wore a contraption on their head that recorded brain activity. Once a mistake occurs, within a quarter of a second, the brain makes two quick symbols. First, an initial response that something is not right, an "oh crap response," according to Moser and his colleagues (2011). The next signal occurs when the person realizes the error and subsequently attempts to correct it. What the study found is that those who produced a bigger second signal—the signal that causes people to recognize the error then try to correct it—are the people who tend to learn from their mistakes. These are the people who can better redirect their thinking to saying, "OK, that wasn't right; now let's see what I need to do to correct it." This group of people took the opportunity to learn from their errors.

When students consciously take the opportunity to learn from all of their errors, they will approach the unsuccessful task in a new way or with more effort. Students who believe that the negative outcome is based on their natural ability will often not bother to try harder after failure; it is then that we hear phrases like, "I am just not good at science," "I will never be able to learn another language," or "It doesn't matter if I do it again, I will have the same results."

Angel Perez, the dean of admission at Pitzer College in California, interviews many students who apply for admission to his institution and always asks potential students the same question, "What do you look forward to the most in college?" On one occasion, he heard a response that took him by surprise: "I look forward to the possibility of failure." This potential student continued, "You see, my parents never let me fail, taking a more rigorous course or trying an activity I may not succeed in, they tell me, it will ruin my chances at college admission" (Perez, 2012, para. 2).

Learning to embrace failure is hardly easy; however, once again, if students learn more about their brain and how it works, failure is an easier pill to swallow. Students who internalize the understanding of the plasticity of the brain and the functional changes in the brain that occur when we learn can deal more constructively with setbacks. They are sometimes even more motivated to work toward mastery and will persist and persevere until they do.

Educators who value the importance of providing challenging opportunities for students find that students react to the challenge in different ways. Some students have a "Bring it on!" approach and embrace the challenge with enthusiasm. These students realize that they may not be successful and might even fail at a task or two, but want to take the risk and stretch themselves. Other students feel threatened by the challenge, are afraid they will not succeed, and will often give up before they put much effort into it.

It is imperative that teachers develop a climate in their classroom where failure is celebrated and students learn to reflect and redirect so that they can approach a challenging task in a new way or with more effort. Teachers can model this behavior themselves in the classroom. The famous entrepreneur and entertainer, Walt Disney, saw the potential for taking risks: "Around here, however, we don't look backwards for very long. We keep moving forward, opening up new doors and doing new things because we're curious, and curiosity keeps leading us down new paths."

Motivation

It is hard to discuss failure without also considering motivation. Social scientist Bernard Weiner (1974, 1980) is best known for his work with attribution theory (see http://education.purduecal.edu/Vockell/EdPsyBook/Edpsy5/edpsy5_attribution.htm for a good overview of attribution theory). Weiner's theory focuses on motivation and achievement and he considers the most important factors affecting achievement to be ability, effort, task difficulty, and luck. Any of those factors sound familiar? Weiner's research on effort was the precursor to growth mindset theory. According to the attribution theory, successful people will often attribute their success to effort, an internal factor. Those who are unsuccessful tend to attribute their lack of success or failure to the difficulty of the task and/or to just having bad luck. (Remember the mention of John McEnroe in Chapter 1? Dweck [2006] uses him throughout her book as an example of a person with a fixed mindset who blamed his failures on external factors like these.) Our goal is to encourage students to internalize the belief that their own actions and behaviors, not external factors, guide them to achievement or failure.

attribution theory

a theory that suggests that successful people will often attribute their success to effort (an internal factor) while those who are unsuccessful tend to attribute their lack of success or failure to the difficulty of the task and/or to just having bad luck (external factors)

In Daniel Pink's 2009 book, *Drive: The Surprising Truth About What Motivates Us*, he presents a good case for intrinsic rather than extrinsic rewards. Intrinsic rewards refer to the personal satisfaction a person feels when something is accomplished, when no outside incentives are in place. Extrinsic rewards come from an outside place, usually a teacher or a parent who promises a "prize," sticker, even money if a child demonstrates success. Pink shows how this can affect a student's performance when he writes,

> In environments where extrinsic rewards are most salient, many people work only to the point that triggers the reward—and no further. So if students get a prize for reading three books, many won't pick up a fourth, let alone embark on a lifetime of reading. (p. 58)

Pink goes on to explain that the practice of trying to motivate by promising rewards has many flaws. Extinguishing student creativity and fostering short-term thinking are a few issues that can surface when students are promised a "reward" to reach a predetermined goal. Instead, the "reward" can be the praise students receive regarding the effort and persistence they put forth coupled with that positive internal feeling that we all get when we have mastered something new. Accomplishing a challenging task is inherently enjoyable.

intrinsic rewards
the personal satisfaction a person feels when something is accomplished

extrinsic rewards
outside incentives provided to a person by another individual or source, such as money, certificates, or prizes

Recent research like Daniel Pink's consistently suggests the value of intrinsic over extrinsic goals for motivation. Another element that has surfaced in literature surrounding motivation is the concept of autonomy, the freedom to decide. As Boykin and Noguera (2011) noted

> Being guided by self-determination, while engaged
> in an activity, results in optimal motivation lev-
> els. It is further postulated that people are more
> self-determined when they feel a sense of auton-
> omy in their pursuits, rather than when they feel
> their pursuits are controlled through coercion,
> external rewards, or guilt/shame avoidance. (p. 84)

With autonomy, there is still accountability, therefore giving
students some level of autonomy should be a consideration in some
situations.

Kou Murayama, a psychological researcher at the University
of California, Los Angeles conducted a study among German students in grades 5–10 (as reported in Blue, 2012). The students were
followed for 5 years, given a math exam and IQ test, and surveyed
about their attitude toward math annually. As a result of this study,
it was found that IQ did not predict new learning. It was the students who were motivated who made the fastest gains. In other
words, those students with a growth mindset! Data captured from
the survey found that those students agreeing with statements such
as, "When doing math, the harder I try, the better I perform" made
more learning gains than students who were bright but not as motivated (Blue, 2012).

Changing How Students React to Failure

When students fail or have many errors, they may look at this
as a sign of weakness and incompetence within themselves, which
can actually lead to more failure. They may begin to avoid anything
that looks remotely challenging so that they do not have to face failure. On the other hand, if students look at failure or errors as a way
to get feedback or reflect on areas that need more attention, they
possess an underlying belief that they will, with effort, persistence,
and help (that they've sought out themselves) eventually grasp the
learning.

Every time teachers help students with an error, they should seize this opportunity to help students interpret the errors as "data" that will help them later, rather than looking at themselves through a lens of low ability. For example, if a student is struggling with solving a math word problem, a teacher should ask the student what strategies she has used and brainstorm some alternative strategies that can be used. Some argue that children from middle- and upper-class homes do not get enough opportunities to fail thanks to well meaning, but highly overprotective adults who catch them before they fall. This is a fine line to walk for parents because if they chose not to step in to prevent failure, then kids may not feel supported and valued.

In 2012, a Canadian teacher was suspended for giving zeros to students who did not turn in work or for tests that were not taken. His school had a strict "no zeroes" policy. He, in turn, believed that students needed to be held accountable for their actions ("Edmonton teacher who gave 0s," 2012). In his 2012 book, *How Children Succeed: Grit, Curiosity, and the Hidden Power of Character,* Paul Tough claimed that grit and persistence are the biggest indicators of student success. He shared that we should be developing a sense of resiliency in the face of failure among our children. The Canadian teacher and Tough both recognized that failure is an important life lesson. However, when faced with failure, it is imperative that opportunities are built in where students can reflect and make adjustments or changes so that they learn from the situation.

One way teachers can help students reflect on failure is to introduce them to a more positive outlook on failure, perhaps by sharing others' attitudes toward failure. For example, cognitive psychologist Jerome Bruner (1961) hit the nail on the head when he framed failure in this way: "Experience success and failure not as a reward and punishment, but as information." (p. 61). Or as a more contemporary figure, Michael Jordan, summed up failure in a 1997 Nike commercial: "I've missed more than 9,000 shots in my career. I've lost almost 300 games. Twenty-six times I've been trusted to take the game-winning shot . . . and missed. I've failed over and over and over again in my life. And that is why I succeed."

Other learning tasks for helping students learn to deal with and accept failure and mistakes can be found in Chapter 8.

CHAPTER 6

WHAT MESSAGES SHOULD PARENTS HEAR ABOUT GROWTH MINDSET?

> "Can you explain the value of failure to my parents?"—Grade 11 student

Another stop along the path to a growth mindset school culture is to develop a plan for sharing information about the malleability of the mind with parents. Even if a school or district is well on its way to developing a growth mindset environment, it is important to get parents educated so that children can hear a consistent message at home.

Parents often struggle with the nature/nurture debate and can attribute a child's success or lack of success to genetics. As clinical psychologist and author Oliver James (2008) stated, "Simply holding the belief that genes largely or wholly determine you or your children can be toxic" (para. 1). He also made the analogy to mental illness, writing, "If you suffer a mental illness, believing it's down to genes means you are less likely to recover, probably because you believe there's nothing you can do about it" (James, 2008, para. 1). Parents, teachers, coaches, scout leaders, and other adult role models should never blame genetics for perceived capabilities. If any adult in a child's life communicates low expectations either verbally or nonverbally, then achievement can suffer.

A secondary outcome of educating parents about malleable intelligence is for themselves. According to Joel F. Wade (2012), author and life coach,

> Adults with growth oriented mindsets are also more likely to engage in more challenging tasks, to persevere and to bounce back from adversity. Management teams with a growth oriented mindset outperform those with a trait-oriented mindset. . . . Also very interesting to note is that people with a growth oriented mindset have a remarkably accurate assessment of their own performance and ability. Those with a fixed mindset have a remarkably inaccurate assessment of their own performance and ability. (para. 16–18)

Information about growth and fixed mindsets, encouraging resilience, basic brain operations, and ways to praise their children are essential concepts that can be shared with parents. In doing so, children will hear a consistent message from adults in their lives that will significantly contribute to developing and maintaining an "I can do this" attitude. This can be done by posting information on the school website, social network sites, newsletter blurbs, principal coffee hours, and/or a parent information evening. (Sample newsletter blurbs in English and Spanish can be found in Appendix B.)

Building Resilience

A central message to communicate with parents is the importance of encouraging resilience in their children. Parents often overlook opportunities for helping children learn to adjust to situations when they are faced with adversity or lack of success. Saying to a child, "No wonder you did not do well on that test, you are always playing video games" or "You shouldn't have tried out for that team in the first place, you knew it would be a long shot" do not contribute to building resilience. Children will eventually try to avoid anything where they are not very sure that they will be successful rather than view the situation as a challenge to arise to. Some suggestions for building resilience in children include:

- *Use growth mindset praise.* Always praise a child's willingness to try, effort, patience, and practice. Do not attribute success to "being smart" or "being the best" but to hard work and perseverance.

- *Model flexibility.* There is an old adage, "We plan and God laughs" and as adults, we know how true that is. Children and teens, on the other hand do not innately have the flexibility or adaptability to always handle a change of plans with grace. Being able to switch gears and change plans is important when building resilience in our children. One of the best things that we can do is to communicate that change is part of living life. Parents can model this for their children by taking a flexible mentality when things do not go their way. For example, if a parent plans a trip to a museum, only to find it's actually closed on Mondays, then he or she could immediately model flexibility by selecting an alternate activity (or offering the kids some alternate activities to choose from). Taking this attitude in everyday life is important as well for parents, especially by not letting frustrating situations get the best of them.

- *Adopt a "glass half full" mentality in the home.* I remember that when my son was once facing a series of setbacks, he morphed into an almost constant "woe is me" mentality. I finally went to the cupboard, took out a glass, filled it halfway, then asked him, "Is this glass half full or half empty?" Given the situation he was in, he responded, "half empty." I asked. "Can you still drink from it? Does it still quench your thirst?" He responded that yes, it still could do both of those things. It was then that I made the analogy to the setbacks he was experiencing. Even during a hardship, we need to find positivity. A child with "hope" believes there can be a positive side to most situations. Parents also need to model a positive attitude, both verbally and nonverbally, when faced with their own setbacks. As far as my son goes, words are no longer necessary—all I have to do is get the glass out of the cupboard, fill it halfway, and set it on the table . . . he gets the message now.

- *Help children find their own niche.* A successful child is a confident child. Sometimes it means trying lots of different things before a child finds an area where she can thrive. This does not mean signing kids up for every lesson, sport, and club that comes along. It means providing opportunities for kids to experience a variety of things: cooking, scrapbooking, chess, stamp collecting, photography . . . you get the picture.

Teaching Parents About the Brain and Growth Mindsets

Just like many educators, parents typically do not have a conceptual understanding of what happens to the brain when learning new things. Educate parents about neural connections so that they can be aware of the importance of practice and persistence. Having the parents participate in some of the student learning experiences that are included in Chapter 8 is also an effective and engaging practice. Students might even be encouraged to take home the materials they create as part of these learning tasks and share them with their parents, explaining to them how their brains work.

Some parents learn best through interactive experiences or discussions on topics. Websites that include videos of neural connections can be found in the Resources section. Parents may also be interested in picking up one of the books in the Resources section, like Dweck's (2006) *Mindset*, Pink's (2009) *Drive*, or Tough's (2012) *How Children Succeed*—all of which are written in a reader-friendly tone, for use in a PTA workshop or book club.

Using popular video clips as a catalyst for getting the conversation started with parents has also proved effective. One especially effective film clip is the interview scene from *The Pursuit of Happyness*. This is the scene where Chris Gardner persuades an interview panel to hire him even though he is wearing a coat with no shirt. Ask parents to observe the verbal and nonverbal actions from Chris Gardner, as well as the businessmen conducting the interview. Focus the discussion on evidence of fixed or growth mindset from the people in the scenes, especially the notion of persistence.

How Can Parents Communicate a Growth Mindset Message to Teachers?

Many parents naturally embrace a growth mindset mentality as simply a part of who they are themselves. Long before the advent of the terms "fixed mindset" and "growth mindset," some parents valued their child's effort and perseverance more than outcome. The conundrum that some of these parents face is that the message is not the same in school. Teachers, counselors, and school administrators could give parents ideas about how to communicate the growth mindset message to a teacher who doesn't subscribe to a similar mindset about success and failure as they do.

Perhaps even, you're a parent reading this book, whose children do not attend a school where a growth mindset environment is practiced. You're looking for ways to bring up the topic with your child's school. I would advise starting with the classroom teacher and personalizing your conversation to your own child's performance. Here are some suggestions about what to say during your conversation with your child's teacher:

1. *Always start with a positive.* Tell the teacher something that your child loves about her class. "Bella loves the way you

read out loud. It is so animated and engaging, it has really piqued her interest in reading."

2. *Share what brings out the best at home.* Include a relationship between resilience, motivation, effort, or other aspects you want to be addressed. Show how this changes the child's performance. Be as specific as possible. For example, "I have found that Bella really responds well when I praise her persistence when working on a homework assignment."

3. *Share what does not work.* Again, keep your own tenets in mind. For example, "I noticed that when I remark on her final product instead of the process/effort she used to get there that she is not as receptive to suggestions"

4. *Establish the partnership.* Make the teacher part of the plan of action that incorporates your beliefs, as well as his or her practices (and both of your best interests for the child). For example, "I would love for us to come up with some common language to use with her so that she will hear a consistent message and work to the best of her ability."

Even though these examples do not specifically use the terms "growth and fixed mindsets," they still philosophically address the elements of a growth mindset. Others cannot change a person's belief system; we can only present ways to allow others to reflect on their beliefs and expectations. Even if a teacher does not have a growth mindset belief system, minimally, the praise language that is used can make a small contribution to a growth mindset culture.

Another area that a parent may want to focus on is access. If a parent feels that his or her child is not having access to challenging learning opportunities due to low expectations from the teacher, this should be discussed. It is possible that the student is right where he or she should be and that the teacher does provide opportunities through both ongoing assessment and student observation. However, it is also possible that a student is not provided with access to higher level learning experiences due to the teacher's perception of the child's intelligence or perhaps the teacher does not have a differentiated classroom where those opportunities exist for any student. This is a more challenging situation for a parent, because communicating the concept of malleable intelligence is not really an appropriate conversation in a parent-teacher conference. However, conversations with the teachers could include some of the following:

- Christopher becomes much more engaged in learning when he feels challenged.
- I noticed that Christopher tends to do better on tasks that require critical thinking—have you noticed the same thing?
- Christopher loves a challenge. I noticed that he is much more motivated when faced with a challenge.
- What does Christopher need to do to have access to some higher level thinking tasks?

Parents need to gauge the level of information to share based on the openness of the teacher and school administrator. At minimum, parents could stop by the principal's office or send an e-mail to a teacher or administrator with a message such as, "I found this really interesting book/article about mindsets and education that you also might find interesting." (An article I like is "Mind-sets and Equitable Education" from the *Principal Leadership* journal, a great synthesis of Dweck's work; see Dweck, 2010, in the reference list for the full information on this article.) Parents can then provide the resources or link to them in an e-mail.

However, things do not always go as planned. For example, during a parent-teacher conference for one of my children, I mentioned to a science teacher that my child did not feel like she could be successful in science due in part to a previous negative experience in science. (The teacher told her that she was just not a science person.) Of course, my hope in sharing that information would be a response that would assure me that he would send positive messages her way, help her anyway that he can, and praise all of the effort she puts forth. Well . . . not so much—his response was . . . wait for it . . ."Oh." Yes, just "Oh."

I then tried to engage him in a discussion about growth mindset. It was a one-sided discussion. I decided then that I would take matters in my own hands and really bump up my efforts in reminding my daughter about malleable intelligence. I had talked to her many, many times about growth mindset, but now it was all about science. I realized a few things during this time—the most important being that students really needed to hear and feel the same message at school. Hearing it from a parent is just not enough. Students need teachers to believe in them as much as their parents do. Another lesson I learned is that if you talk to a 12–year-old about the same thing ad nauseam, then you will get "the hand" . . . as in the "Stop, I have heard this from you a thousand times before and it is not helping" hand gesture. In hindsight, I should have arranged another meeting with her teacher (with research on mindsets in hand) to make one last attempt to share the research about malleable intelligence and hopefully adjust his messaging to "effort" praise when responding to students' performance in science.

In situations where teachers are just not "buying" the whole growth mindset/malleable intelligence theory, all we can ask is for them to, at the very least, send messages that value effort. A principal once shared that he had a member of his staff who did not believe in the growth and fixed mindset research. She believed that she only ever had a few highly able students in her classroom each year. She remarked that most years the majority of her class was "average" and "below average." The principal asked her to continue to talk to her colleagues, gave her some additional resources on neuroplasticity and growth mindset, and offered to continue the discussion with her. But in the meantime, he asked her to do two things. First, he asked that she only use growth mindset praise in her classroom, to praise what a student does, not who a student is—in other words, to focus on effort-based praise. Second, he asked this teacher to give all students opportunities to participate in higher level learning experiences, even if she did not think the students were "ready" for it. Even though the teacher did not embrace growth mindset, she was asked to put some things in place that might positively affect her students. This is by no means the ideal, simply a bandage until the

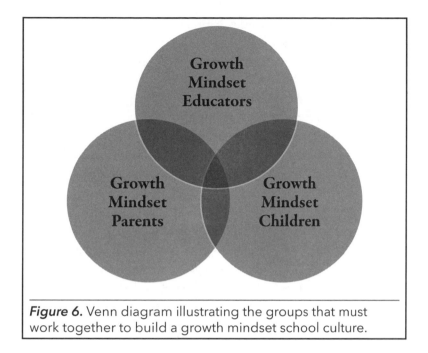

Figure 6. Venn diagram illustrating the groups that must work together to build a growth mindset school culture.

teacher embraces the concept. Because I have a growth mindset, I do believe that with effort, persistence, and the right people collaborating with her, she will eventually adopt a growth mindset.

The diagram in Figure 6 illustrates the importance of all three groups—students, teachers, and parents—to work together when building a growth mindset culture. The most important of these is the adopting of and maintaining of a growth mindset in children.

Get Feedback From Parents

After a "Growth Mindset Parents Information Night" in one district, comments were gathered in order to capture what parents were thinking and planning based on the information they heard. Here are a few of the comments that they shared:

- "I am thinking about my son who achieves with minimal effort; now in seventh grade, material is becoming more difficult and more effort is required. I need to facilitate his growth mindset while maintaining his confidence. He likes having natural effortless perfection."

- "I don't encourage a growth mindset for math with my daughter, she says she doesn't like math and she isn't good at it. I don't disagree with her. I need to be more patient when things are difficult for her."

- "I need to really evaluate the way I praise my children. I need to have more self-controlled thinking before I speak. I am very proud of the efforts of all of my children but I am not sure they know it right now."

Gathering written feedback from parents after a growth mindset information session will give you data that will help inform your next session. A half sheet of paper with two simple statements ("As a result of this session, I am thinking . . ." and "As a result of this session, I am planning . . .") can provide a lot of meaningful information. You could also have parents take on a task similar to the one given to teachers in professional development sessions (see Chapter 2). Have them write down what they believe about intelligence before the workshop, then have them compare their answers after the workshop's conclusion. They can then apply what they've learned to how they might change their approaches when talking with their children.

Providing information to parents about the importance of effort and persistence should be ongoing. Students can also be charged with interviewing their parents about their beliefs regarding intelligence. Children may, in fact, be the catalysts for helping their parents truly understand the malleability of the mind.

CHAPTER 7

CAN GIFTED EDUCATION AND A GROWTH MINDSET BELIEF COEXIST?

"I am learning not to give up if I fail a test."–Grade 10 student

The National Association of Gifted Children (NAGC) convened a group of scholars and practitioners for The National Summit on Low-Income, High Ability Learners in May 2012. The result of this summit was the publication of the report compiled by Paula Olszewski-Kubilius and Jane Clarenbach, *Unlocking Emergent Talent: Supporting High Achievement of Low-Income, High-Ability Students* (see http://www.nagc. org/uploadedFiles/Conventions_and_Seminars/National_ Research_Summit/Unlocking%20Emergent%20Talent%20 FULL%20No-Tint.pdf for a copy of the report). One of the key issues discussed during this summit were the barriers to participation in advanced programs. It was concluded that one of the main reasons that barriers exist is due to a conception of giftedness that emphasizes and values only already developed ability. If a school or system weighs already developed ability, talent, or performance heavily when considering students for identification or participation in advanced programs, many students will be overlooked. According to the report,

> This process often fails to identify children who are less likely to live in a literacy-rich home and community where reading, writing, and language are understood to be critical for academic success. In many cases, otherwise capable children may not be able to demonstrate their advanced learning potential on a test or other performance assessments until after they have access to challenging curriculum and enriched learning opportunities. (Olszewski-Kubilius & Clarenbach, 2012, p. 9)

Think about that last phrase—"access to challenging curriculum and enriched learning opportunities." Are students in your school or district allowed these opportunities if they do not exhibit already developed abilities? What are some ways that your school or district can allow for access of challenging instructional experiences for all students, especially those with potential or motivation to succeed?

The Gifted Label

Let's now think about the practice of labeling a child "gifted." Doesn't telling a child that she is "gifted" manifest a fixed mindset? This goes back to the importance of growth mindset praise. Growth mindset praise is about praising what the child does, not who the child is. We never want to say, "You are so smart" but saying, "You are gifted" sends the same message—it says that the child has permanent traits and that those traits are being judged. Carol Dweck explained it this way:

To the extent that young people believe they simply have a gift that makes them intelligent or talented, they may not put in the work necessary to sustain that talent, moreover, the gifted label that many students still receive, and that their parents relish, may turn some children into students who are overly cautious and challenge-avoidant lest they make mistakes and no longer merit the label. (as quoted in Horowitz, Subotnik, & Matthews, 2009, p. xii)

During a keynote address to Baltimore County, MD, educators in May 2012, Carol Dweck also shared that "Too much emphasis on who is gifted creates kids who think they have to be infallible." Does the practice of identifying gifted students and grouping them together contribute to a growth mindset culture? What message do these practices send to the students deemed "gifted" as well as the rest of the student population?

Former science teacher and university professor, Debbie Silver, author of 2012's *Fall Down 7 Times Get Up 8* shares an experience that she had when her own son was identified as gifted. She felt proud when he was selected into a new gifted and talented program when he was in fourth grade. However, she observed that his participation in the program promoted a sense of entitlement that made him feel like he was smarter than everyone else:

Occasionally, I overheard some of the kids in his gifted class make disparaging remarks about their peers who were "not so bright." I think designers of G/T programs need to be heedful of mindsets and be cautious about encouraging growth rather than fixed mindsets in learners. (p. 89)

Silver (2012) went on to say that she felt that her son was not really able to enjoy the process of learning like most students due to feeling that he always had to "live up to the expectations about him

87

always being the best—at everything. He mostly liked games that he could repeatedly win, and he quickly lost interest in areas where he was not immediately superior" (p. 89).

The October 2012 edition of *Gifted Child Quarterly* contained the article, *A Proposed Direction Forward for Gifted Education Based on Psychological Science.* The authors (Subotnik, Olszewski-Kubilius, & Worrell, 2012) provided much food for thought regarding present practices in gifted education; perhaps one of the more notable points mirrors a growth mindset belief: "What determines whether individuals are gifted or not is not what they are but what they do" (p. 180). An homage to effort. The authors interpretation of giftedness continued, noting that, "There is growing literature on the importance of talent development, one can argue that giftedness in children is probably best described as potential" (Subotnik et al., p. 180). The authors then described a continuum of development that begins with potential, grows to achievement (which is where many measure the "giftedness"), and may or may not result in completely developed talents or, as the authors call it, "eminence." At each stage of development, instruction must be responsive to student needs. At the third stage, eminence, the learner must have opportunities to develop in his or her areas of strengths and areas of domain-specific abilities in unique ways. The authors suggest that these domain-specific strengths should be the areas that educators help develop further, even if this means introducing typical high school content in middle school and middle school content in elementary school.

Thinking about the research noted above, educators and parents must be careful about throwing around the gifted and talented (GT) label. First of all, one could argue that all children possess "gifts" and/or "talents" in a myriad of traditional and nontraditional areas. When educators chose to use the term *gifted*, it should be used in moderation. Perhaps when a student reaches the stage of eminence (Subotnik et al., 2012) or when the child is an outlier within his age peer group and his instructional needs are so far beyond what is typically available that a very different instructional setting is needed, then the gifted label may be applied.

In a 2011 interview with University of California at Berkeley researcher, Frank Worrell, he described giftedness as something that is "rare or uncommon." He expanded on this by explaining,

> A child of four who can write decent poetry may be considered a gifted writer, whereas the same quality of poetry being produced by an adolescent would not be considered gifted. The four-year old's performance is rare even compared to other outstanding four year olds, but poetry writing among adolescents is too common among adolescents for merely decent poetry to make the grade. An adolescent would need to produce critically acclaimed poetry to be considered gifted. Similarly, a student beginning an undergraduate degree at age 13 may be considered gifted whereas an 18-year-old beginning a college degree is not considered gifted. Finally, only a small number of individuals get drafted to national sports leagues every year, but we typically only consider the top draft picks as the gifted individuals, despite the fact that being drafted is itself a rare phenomenon.
>
> In sum, the term, gifted is applied to accomplishments that are rare and superior even when compared to others who have made outstanding accomplishments in a domain. (Young, 2011, para. 5–6)

Rather than overusing the term gifted, consider using other words or phrases such as "high-potential learners" or "highly motivated." Everyone has potential that needs to be nurtured so consider overusing the word "potential" (not "possible") rather than the word "gifted." Also, it's important to note that the GT label becomes unimportant when students' instructional needs are being met consistently. Schools must adopt a differentiated, responsive instruction model as described in Chapter 3. Educators must work toward developing the talent in each and every child. If the needs of the students are being responded to within the course of instruction, then the need for a separate grouping of perceived GT students becomes less important.

Early Ability Grouping

Thankfully, the majority of school districts across the country do not begin to subjectively sort kids into separate, self-contained GT classes in every neighborhood school at the elementary level. Those that do are providing a disservice to their young students, both those in the gifted class and those who are not. For the elementary students placed in a gifted class, the situation perpetuates a fixed mindset—"I am smart, therefore I better not fail"—and in many cases, these students will avoid opportunities for intellectual risk taking just as Debbie Silver described her fourth-grade son doing. What message does this structure send to the students not placed in the gifted class?

Here's one example of the negative messages such a structure creates that I experienced. At a suburban school, three classes of grade 4 students were formed. Two of these classes were called "GT 4th Grade"; the final class was for all of the other students. Many savvy parents advocated for their students to be in a GT class and would do whatever they could to get on the "GT train." This district had a subjective process in place that did not include a cognitive assessment and weighed already developed ability heavily. The curriculum for this class was separate than the on-level class in the four major content areas: reading, math, social studies, and science.

The parent of one of the students in the on-level class called the school system's GT office to share her daughter, Rosa's, experience in the on-level class. You might initially think that she was calling to get her child into the GT class; this was not the case, as the parent felt that an on-level class with differentiation was the appropriate placement for her daughter. Instead, the parent reported that, since the addition of the GT classes at fourth grade, Rosa had experienced many changes, particularly in the way she perceived student expectations. Rosa perceived that all of the smart kids must be in the other two classes and therefore she was not viewed as capable by the teachers in her school. Rosa's view (and perhaps this is shared by the teachers at her school) was that her teachers did not have very high expectations of her, as well as of the other students in her class. She did not believe that she could get smarter, not even if she tried her very best. Rosa had been put on a track and this track caused her to believe that she would not have access to different, more challenging instructional opportunities. For the students not grouped in the GT class, the message was loud and clear: "We do not expect much from you."

The parents of some "gifted" students might argue that GT classes at the elementary level should not only exist but be exclusive due to perceptions that other students, who may not have yet developed their ability fully, may slow down their own children. They believe that policies and philosophies should be customized to those students who learn quickly, were born "smart," or have already "arrived." The GT policies in many school districts contribute to a fixed mindset mentality. These policies cause students, parents, and educators to believe that sorting kids at an early age is a good practice. It is not. Responding to the *instructional needs* of students at a young age is. Students need to continually be observed and evaluated through a lens of potential and possibilities. Educators must learn to recognize sparks and provide appropriate challenge. Children should have access to challenging instruction whenever they need it, at every grade level, in every content area.

With that said, there are a few elementary students who need an instructional setting that will allow them to further develop their gifts and talents. These are those "rare or uncommon" children that Dr. Worrell speaks of (Young, 2011). All students need an intellectual peer group. This is especially true when the student is an outlier in his or her abilities. Schools and systems do need to think about solutions for meeting the needs of students who lack an intellectual peer group in their neighborhood school. If it is a midsized or large district, then creation of a center for these outliers or highly gifted students should be considered. Perhaps beginning at grades 4 and 5, classroom(s) could be set up in a central location for those students whose needs cannot be met at their local school. These centers could provide what these students need instructionally and offer opportunities to develop domain-specific strengths more deeply. They could also provide an intellectual peer group and should be staffed with teachers with endorsement or certification in gifted education. In addition, the social and emotional needs of these students cannot be ignored. It is imperative that a counselor is on staff who possesses the expertise in the social and emotional challenges that these outliers may face. These challenges include but are not limited to issues surrounding asynchronous development, overexcitabilities, and perfectionism.

Wherever students are being educated, differentiated, responsive teaching strategies should be in place as a range of background knowledge, opportunities, and abilities exist in these settings as well. I remember receiving a phone call from a principal who was concerned about a child placed in a gifted class. The child was falling behind, and the principal was considering removing him from the class. In order to gain more information, I began asking questions. One of the first questions that I asked was about differentiation—how the child did on preassessments. I also asked about the flexible grouping practices within the classroom. The principal responded with, "Didn't you hear me? I said it was a GT class. We don't differentiate in our GT classes." That response spoke volumes to me about how some educators view classes with highly able learners . . . they treat everyone the same.

At the elementary level, the majority of students' needs should be met in responsive, differentiated classrooms with flexible instructional groups. At the middle school level, the enrollment is typically larger and the probability of having an intellectual peer group is greater than elementary school; therefore, instructional choices should be available such as "Standard" and "Advanced," "Accelerated," "Enriched," or "Honors" courses (note, no classes labeled "Gifted"). The expectation must exist that differentiated, responsive instruction will occur in all levels of courses. See Chapter 3 for an overview of ways to create differentiated, responsive instruction in all classrooms.

If students believe that they will, with effort and persistence, be successful in environments of challenging instruction, they are more likely to succeed. This is validated by findings in the NAGC *Unlocking Emergent Talent* report: "If students believe that they are welcome in advanced courses and teachers expect them to do well, they are more likely to bounce back from setbacks with increased effort and persistence" (Olszewski-Kubilius & Clarenbach, 2012, p. 17).

Your Philosophy for Gifted Education

Reflect on the GT philosophy in your own school or school district. If you do not currently have a philosophy, consider building one that includes the following:

- A conception of giftedness that emphasizes potential and possibilities. Use words and phrases like: access, potential, develop, nurture, motivation, *all* students, responsive, beliefs, talent development, and expectations.
- Curriculum development that embeds preassessment and formative assessment, as well as practices and strategies that develop and observe talent/potential including critical and creative thinking.
- Identification processes for recognition of potential that are inclusive, use a variety of criteria, use local norms, are ongoing, and do not rely on referrals or nominations— data should be collected on *all* students, not just those who are referred. This process should embed direct instructional implications and not be a "stand-alone" process.
- Recognition of what students need and how these needs will be responded to both instructionally as well as social-emotionally. The GT label is unimportant, the philosophy should be about responding to academic needs.
- Differentiated/responsive instruction that always allows for the possibility of enrichment and topic/content acceleration for all students. Remember, it is about access for all, not just those with a label.

A philosophy of gifted education in a school or district that has adopted a growth mindset might sound like this:

Students in Pre-K–Grade 12 will have:
- Curriculum that embeds strategies that will develop potential, allow for development of talent, infuse 21st-century learning skills, and nurture creative and critical cognitive abilities in all students;
- Access to enriched and accelerated instructional opportunities for all students, specifically those with the capability, potential, and/or motivation to embrace the challenge;
- instruction that is responsive to the needs of all students, which includes preassessment, curriculum compacting, flexible cluster grouping, rigorous enrichment and acceleration experiences, and differentiated formative and summative assessments; and
- educators who have adopted a belief system where they embrace a growth mindset about the malleability of the mind and have internalized neuroscience research that proves that everyone can get "smarter" with a proper instructional menu coupled with persistence, effort, and motivation of the learner.

For those students who are truly outliers:
- An instructional setting for those students who demonstrate profound, exceptional ability when compared with others of their age, experience, or environment and who have needs that cannot be met in a regular classroom setting.

Notice anything about the sample above? "Gifted" is not mentioned specifically at all. What has been developed is not just a gifted philosophy, but a teaching and learning philosophy for all students that addresses differentiated responsive instruction, curriculum development, and teacher beliefs/expectations. With the exception of the last bullet that addresses the need for an intellectual peer group for outliers, all of the other bullets are just about strong, differentiated, responsive instruction—something that every student is entitled to. The goal of every school or district is to develop an instructional philosophy that addresses the needs of our most advance learners while at the same time allowing access to instruction to all learners.

CHAPTER 8

WHAT ARE SOME WAYS TO HELP STUDENTS ADOPT A GROWTH MINDSET?

"I felt my brain growing when I was doing that game"–Grade 3 student

More and more studies are surfacing that emphasize the importance of teaching students about their own brains. Increase of motivation, willingness to accept new challenges, and healthier reaction to failure are only a few of the benefits a child will experience when he or she understands how his or her brain works. With tight curriculum mapping and school systems' emphasis on consistent educational experiences among grade-level and content-area classes, educators are losing the flexibility to "add on" anything more to an already very crowded curriculum and instruction plan. Therefore creativity is needed when looking for ways to embed some conceptual neuroscience and growth mindset knowledge into the instructional day.

Please keep in mind that this is not a one-lesson experience—students need to be constantly reminded that they have the ability to get smarter and that each and every brain has an elastic quality to it. It all depends on how you use it. Therefore, we need to get creative about ways to teach and revisit the concept of malleable intelligence. Begin to think about the subject area and grade level that you teach. Where are the opportunities to introduce some basic brain education? If you teach reading or English, consider choosing a nonfiction text about neuroscience or learning and the brain when exploring comprehension strategies for expository texts. English teachers can also highlight characters who exhibit growth or fixed mindset traits (look at the Analyzing Authors and Characters Sample Learning Task later in this chapter as a guide). Science educators can begin the school year with a mini-unit or weave a thread of neuroscience through an entire year of biology.

Learning Sequence

On the following pages, ideas can be found for building a conceptual understanding of the brain, as well as fixed and growth mindset tasks for students. Following a responsive instruction model, each section will list several ideas for teachers to use with their students. Some can be used across many grade levels due to the open-endedness of the strategy or task. Others are learning tasks that are specific to grade levels. Use this as a menu and pick and choose learning opportunities that will be the most beneficial to your students.

Preview and Preassessment (Activate Background Knowledge)

As mentioned in Chapter 3, in order to plan for effective, differentiated instruction, we must first activate background knowledge and find out what students already know about the brain and how it functions.

Elementary Preview

The preassessment preview for elementary students might be as simple as a series of questions that initiate a discussion like the following:

- Teacher points to his or her head and says:
  - ○ "Who knows what is in here?"
  - ○ "What do we use our brain for?"

Middle and High School Preview

Secondary students can actively take part in a discussion about the brain to help their teachers gauge their knowledge. Show students a picture of the brain and have a 2–3 minute discussion about the brain, allowing them to contribute information as the conversation flows.

Elementary Preassessment

Teachers should explain to the students that they would like to find out what the students already know about the brain and how it functions. For example, you could say, "I am going to give you a paper, and I would like for you to do two things." Hold up a copy of the blank preassessment for the brain (see Figure 7) and ask the students, "Who can tell me what shape these dots are forming?" (expect answers such as head or face).

Distribute the preassessment found in Figure 7. Ask students to draw a picture of what they think their brains might look like inside the blank outline of the head. Then, students should write down anything that they know about their brain. Remind students that this is not for a grade, but just to gauge their knowledge.

After the students have completed the preassessments, review them, looking for patterns of responses. Common responses include:

99

Name _____ Date _____

Draw a picture of what you think your brain looks like.

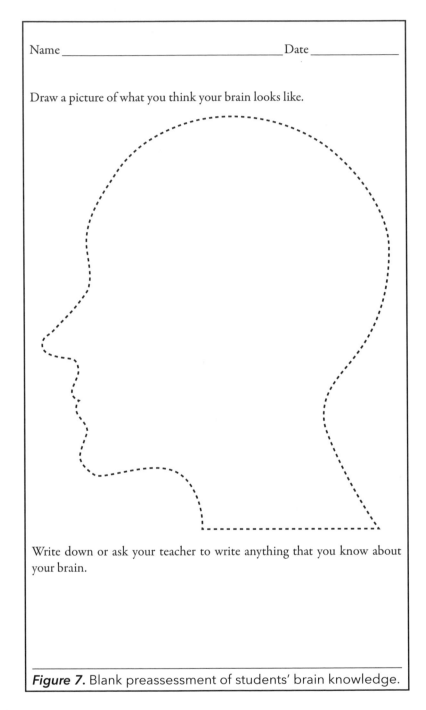

Write down or ask your teacher to write anything that you know about your brain.

Figure 7. Blank preassessment of students' brain knowledge.

- "My brain helps me think."
- "My brain makes me smart."

Also analyze the students' drawings of the brain: Is the size accurate? Make generalizations about the student's baseline knowledge about the brain. Make note of any student(s) who seem to have more than basic knowledge about the brain and plan for differentiation for these students (such as the completed assessments for Mike, Devin, and Alana in Figures 8–10). Other students will have some knowledge of their brains but need more information about how the brain works. Some will simply be starting at square one and need much more instruction.

Middle and High School Preassessment

You can either give students a similar preassessment to the one in Figure 7 or students can simply jot down their ideas to the question: "Share everything that you know about the human brain."

Why Preassess? Will Students Really Know Much About the Brain?

At any grade level, the preassessment will serve as a way for teachers to find out just exactly where they need to begin. While preparing to give the above mentioned preassessment to a group of Grade 3 students, their teacher remarked that it was probably a waste of time because the students didn't know anything about the brain. In some cases, yes, the preassessment will demonstrate little to no understanding. I've had students respond simply with "My brain helps me think" coupled with a drawing of some scribbles or a spaghetti-like mass. Keep in mind that the purpose of a preassessment is so that you can match students' instruction to their needs—how will you know which students fall in the category of knowing much about their brain and which ones need more instruction without ever administering the preassessment? It's never a waste of time!

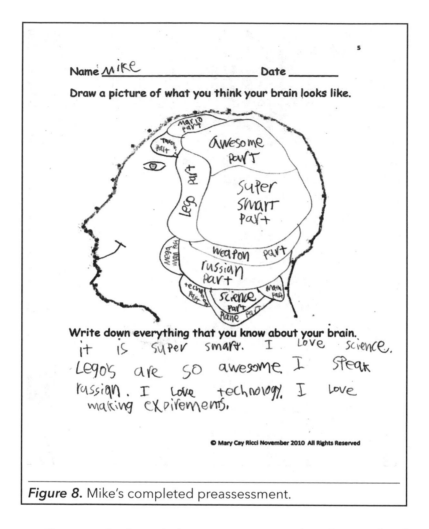

Name Mike _____ Date _____

Draw a picture of what you think your brain looks like.

Write down everything that you know about your brain.

it is super smart. I love science.
Lego's are so awesome. I speak
russian. I love technology. I love
making expirements.

Figure 8. Mike's completed preassessment.

For example, through this process, many students have surfaced in all grade levels that show some understanding of brain function. Take a look at Vierra's brain preassessment in Figure 11.

An interesting thing happened when I was visiting Vierra's third-grade classroom and administering the preassessment. Students were sitting at about six per table, and I was walking around observing when I noticed Vierra hunched over, pencil in hand, writing copiously on her paper. I stopped behind her for just a moment to take a look at what she was writing. No sooner had I stopped when

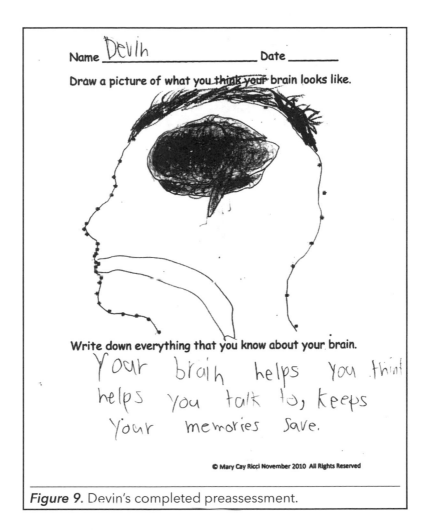

Name Devin _____ Date _____

Draw a picture of what you think your brain looks like.

Write down everything that you know about your brain.

Your brain helps you think helps you talk to, keeps your memories save.

Figure 9. Devin's completed preassessment.

one of the boys at the table announced: "Yes, look at her paper, she is the smart one." I assured him that he and all of the children at his table were working hard on the task and doing a good job. He thought about that for a minute and said, "Yeah, but she is still the smart one." I knew then that a lot of work was to be done to build a growth mindset culture in this classroom.

When I was evaluating the preassessments, Vierra's certainly did stand out so I asked her teacher if I could speak to this student for a few minutes. I complemented Vierra on her hard work and

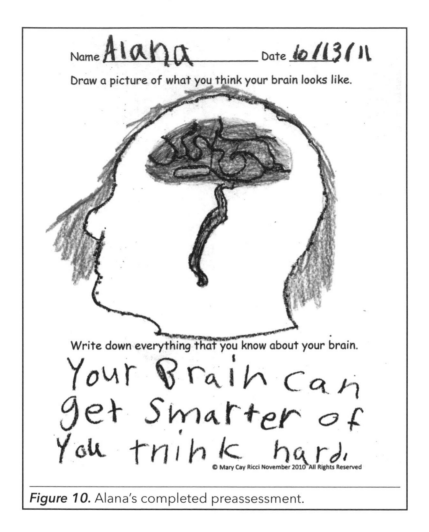

Name **Alana**   Date **6/13/11**

Draw a picture of what you think your brain looks like.

Write down everything that you know about your brain.

Your Brain can get smarter of You thihk hard.

© Mary Cay Ricci November 2010 All Rights Reserved

Figure 10. Alana's completed preassessment.

asked her where she learned so much about the brain. She explained that her grandmother was a doctor, and she had learned from her.

I also questioned a first-grade student about a response that was shared on his preassessment. The child wrote that the brain was the place that "keeps the card in." After questioning the student, it was determined that he was referring to a memory card like those found in a digital camera or some video game devices—a place that stores all of your information. Talk about a 21st-century response!

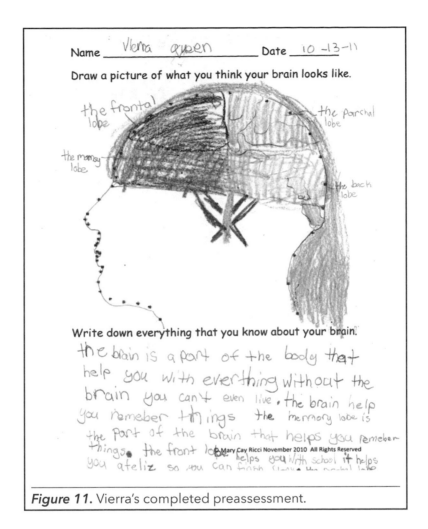

Name ___Vierra green___ Date ___10 -13-11___

Draw a picture of what you think your brain looks like.

the frontal lobe

the parchal lobe

the mamay lobe

the back lobe

Write down everything that you know about your brain.

the brain is a part of the body that help you with everthing without the brain you can't even live. the brain help you remeber things the memory lobe is the part of the brain that helps you remeber things. the front lobe helps you with school it helps you ateliz so you can finish...the parchal lobe

Figure 11. Vierra's completed preassessment.

Preassess Growth Mindset and Fixed Mindset

Share with students a few common responses from the preassessment on the brain. For example, tell students "You worked hard on your 'brain papers.' Many of you said that your brain helps you think!" Explain that they will be learning more about the brain but first you would like to get their opinions on a few statements. Students can use "agree/disagree" signs or thumbs up/thumbs down to respond to the following three statements. These statements are adapted from Carol Dweck's Mindset Works (http://www.mindsetworks.com) workshop.

Tell students, "I am going to read and show you a few sentences. If you agree with them, then hold up your agree sign and if you disagree, then hold up your disagree sign. Don't worry about what others are doing; I want to know what *you* think!" Take note on who agrees and disagrees with the following statements:

- Everyone can learn new things. (Growth Mindset Belief)
- Some kids are born smarter than others. (Fixed Mindset Belief)
- We can change how smart we are. (Growth Mindset Belief)

We expect that all students should agree with the statement "Everyone can learn new things." What needs to be noted are the responses to "We can change how smart we are" and "Some kids are born smarter than others." If students agree with the latter statement, then chances are they have a fixed mindset when it comes to their own potential. As discussed in Chapter 1, we found that the older the child, the more likely that he or she had a fixed mindset in some aspect of learning. You may also want to interview some students privately to find out about their mindset, particularly if you suspect the answer was not authentic. Or if you feel the need to make the reactions more anonymous, have students put their heads on their desks and then provide a thumbs up sign when they agree and a thumbs down when they disagree.

Once you've preassessed the students you're working with for both their knowledge of the brain and their thoughts on mindset, you can implement the sample learning tasks I describe in the next few sections.

Sample Learning Task #1: The Brain Is Like a Sponge (All Grade Levels)

"I know that my brain grows like a sponge and I have to exercise my brain like my body."—Grade 4 student

Attributes of a _____

Attributes of a _____	?

Figure 12. Chart used with Guess Box activity.

This learning task utilizes the Guess Box Strategy, based on the Concept Attainment Model developed by Jerome Bruner. This model is a teaching approach that helps students develop skills for *inductive* and *deductive* thinking. This can be done while learning content in any field in a constructive and meaningful way. A box in which the contents are unknown is a good vehicle for concept attainment and critical thinking. Prior to the lesson, set up one wide column and one thin column on the board or chart paper. At the top of the wide column, write "Attributes of a _____." At the top of the thinner column place a question mark (see Figure 12).

Let the students know that their task is to find out what is in the box. They may only ask questions that can be answered with a "yes" or a "no." Make it clear that the "no" answers are just as important as the "yes" answers because they give us valuable information about the item's attributes. As students learn about the item's attributes through their questioning, record all of the positive attributes on the chart paper. There is no limit as to the number of questions that the students can ask. In fact, it is when many of the students know what is in the box that the questioning becomes higher level and the teacher begins to recognize "sparks" in his or her students. Many teachers end the Guess Box strategy as soon as they think a few kids know what is in it, hence, students miss out on an opportunity to really conceptualize what the object represents.

It is very important to debrief and reflect on the Guess Box process after the item is revealed. Ask students the following:

- What question helped you (the most) to figure out what was in the box?
- Who asked that question? Why did you ask it?

Find out why students asked specific questions. Discuss with students which questions were important to them and why. What kind of information was gained by these questions?

- What are the three most valuable attributes? In other words, if we could only choose three of these words or phrases to describe this object, what would they be?

If students disagree, discuss the information that was gained with each attribute and come to a consensus. Strategies like Guess Box contribute to a growth mindset culture. Students who surface with well-thought-out questions can often be those students who may not shine in more traditional areas of school.

Once students are familiar with the process of the Guess Box activity, use it to facilitate new learning about the brain using the Guess Box: Let's Get Your Brain Working! lesson described in the next section.

Guess Box: Let's Get Your Brain Working!

Put a dry, flat sponge in a guess box. If possible, use a flattened "pop up" sponge that expands or changes shape when it gets wet. Set up the chart paper with two columns: "Attributes of a _____" and a question mark. Tell the students:

> This is something that comes in a lot of different colors so you do not have to ask any questions about color. (You may want to add that many are yellow.) This is something that you might use when you clean.

Then allow the children to ask questions to try to determine what's in the box. After students have asked many questions about the mystery object in the box, the chart should list the attributes

Kindergarten	First Grade	Second Grade
Use it to clean	Use it to clean	Use it to clean
Many are yellow	It is usually a rectangle	It is usually a rectangular prism
It is in your house	You can find it in the kitchen	Use it to wash dishes
Usually in the bathroom	It can clean a hard floor	It has six faces
Usually in the kitchen	A person makes it work	Use it to clean the floor
It is squishy	It is sometimes soft	It is squishy
It can be hard	You can rip it	It has holes in it
It is usually a rectangle	You can use it to wipe	Use it with soap
It can get wet	It needs water	You need to wet it
It feels bumpy	You can use it with cleaning spray	
You can dry it		

Figure 13. Attributes of a sponge listed as part of the Guess Box: Let's Get Your Brain Working! learning task.

that helped students come to the conclusion that a sponge was in the box. Figure 13 includes examples of the charts from kindergarten, first-, and second-grade classrooms I worked with. These attributes are listed as a result of the questions that the students asked.

After students determine that a sponge is in the box and they debrief the process they use to get there, pose this question: "How is your brain like a sponge?" Ask students to think about things that are the same when thinking about a sponge and a brain. Actual student responses have included:

- They are both pink.
- They are both squishy.
- They both grow.
- They both absorb.

Now, set up the following scenario for students:

> Let's take a look at our sponge again. I am putting it in this jar, and I am going to slowly add water to it. Now it is time to use your imagination: Let's pretend that the sponge is your brain and the water represents all of the new things you learn every day. What do you think will happen to your brain when you add all of the new things that you learn?

Slowly pour water over the sponge. The students will see how the sponge begins to grow and absorb the water. Tell them, "Every time you work hard and learn something new your brain grows and gets stronger. The sponge is bigger and will now work better since it is wet." Students can then observe what happens to the sponge over several days without water: It begins to dry and shrivel. Relate this to what happens to a brain when it is not being challenged.

Sample Learning Task #2: Building a Neural Network

"If work gets hard, I just imagine neurons in my brain trying to connect."—Grade 5 student

Several ideas are provided below to help students build a conceptual understanding of what happens in the brain when they learn. These explanations also help students visualize the neural connections that are made and strengthened with learning, practice, and mastery.

Before you share these learning experiences, give students some background on how the brain works, telling them, "Inside the brain we all have brain cells called *neurons*. We have billions of neurons, some connect to each other and some are just sort of floating around." Show them a picture or diagram of a neuron, like the one in Figure 14. Ask students to think about what might cause these

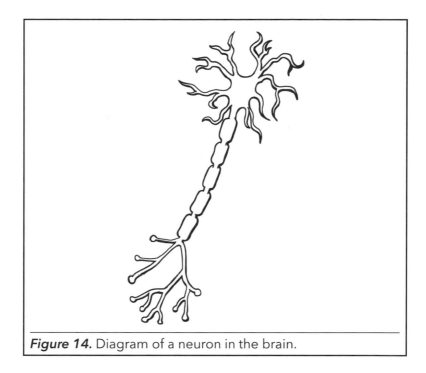

Figure 14. Diagram of a neuron in the brain.

neurons to connect with each other. Here are a few sample learning experiences that can help you teach students this concept:

1. *Learning Experience #1: Students Become Neurons.*
   - Ask for three to five students to volunteer to be neurons. With elementary and middle school students, you can have them hold a picture of a neuron or hang a cardstock neuron around their neck.
   - Ask the students if someone could share something new that he or she learned recently. Responses might include multiplication, a foreign language, sewing, a sport, and so on. For illustrative purposes, we will choose Sam's response. Sam shared that he just learned how to divide in math class. Announce that this group of neurons now represents part of Sam's brain.
   - Take a thin piece of thread and ask two of the student neurons to connect using this thread, with each of them holding one end. This thin connection will

represent division. Explain to the students that Sam is just beginning to learn how to divide, so this is a weak connection.

- Ask Sam if there is something that he has learned and that he is getting better at but still might need some practice. In this case, let's say that Sam responds with "multiplication." At that point, two of the student neurons can connect using a thicker connection such as a piece of yarn. This represents a better understanding of multiplication than division, but it is not yet at mastery level.

- Then propose the following scenario: Let's look at Sam's division connection: It is represented by a thin piece of thread, but what will happen to this connection after Sam has more experience learning about and practicing division? Let's say that Sam persists and puts forth a lot of effort and eventually becomes an expert in division. How will this connection change? At this point demonstrate how this thread of a connection is replaced with a strong, thick rope. (Macramé cording works well here.) See Figures 15 and 16 for examples of how this lesson was implemented in two classrooms.

- What if, instead, Sam decides that division is just too hard for him and he gives up? What will happen to this connection? (It will stay a weak connection or disconnect entirely.)

- Ask students to think of a time when they felt frustrated learning something new. Ask them to visualize their neurons making stronger connections every time they push through the challenge and master new learning. Tell them to think about these neural connections when they are faced with a challenge. Remind them, "Once you build a strong connection, you have added density to your brain and actually made yourself smarter!"

Figure 15. Students in Betsy Book's first-grade class at Randallstown Elementary School in Maryland demonstrate neural connections. Photo by Ken Myers.

Figure 16. Grade 1 students in Farrah Connelly's class discuss which connections are strong (the thick cording) and which connections represent a new learning (thin piece of thread). Photo by Ken Myers.

- You may also ask students to draw their strong and weak or "not yet" neural connections. Draw a rough shape of the brain on a piece of paper and ask students to think about things they understand and are very good at as well as things that they are just learning, but "not yet" understanding fully. Figures 17 and 18 share few examples of Grade 1 students' neural connections. Take a look at Figure 17. Kamaren's brain shows very strong neural connections for math, spelling, and riding his dirt bike. He explained however, that his strongest connection is "bugging my mother"—he felt he was very good at that!

2. *Learning Experience #2: Road Map.* Make an analogy to destinations and roads to explain the connection between neurons and the brain. For example, draw a picture of the school on the board, then ask students how they might get from the school to their home, to the store, to a gas station, and so on. Then show how they can move from that location to another one. Each location (neuron) has a connection or path to another destination. You can use the map in Figure 19 to help you demonstrate this to your class. Tell students,

   "Some have connections to a lot of different locations and others are weaker because you don't travel to that particular destination often. When you learn a new route, or a new road is built, this makes new connections. Neurons work in a similar way. They make hundreds of connections. The more you learn, the more connections are made. The more they are traveled, the stronger the learning."

3. *Learning Experience #3: Visualization.* Ask students to visualize walking through an unexplored forest. You can

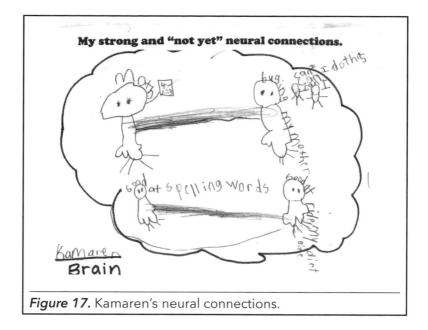

Figure 17. Kamaren's neural connections.

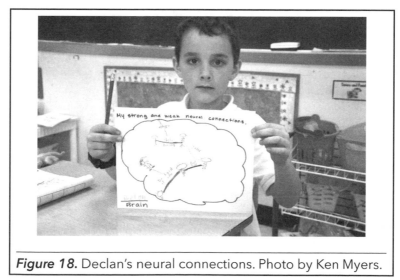

Figure 18. Declan's neural connections. Photo by Ken Myers.

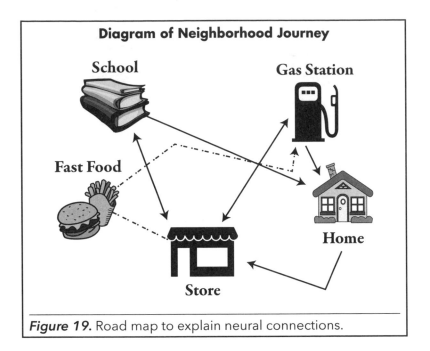

Figure 19. Road map to explain neural connections.

use this script as you walk them through their visualization session:

"There are no paths, no plants that have been trampled on, nothing to lead the way. A new neural pathway is like walking through an unexplored forest for the first time. The more frequently the path is used, the fewer the barriers and obstacles that stand in the way. Eventually a clear path is created. That clear path represents a clear understanding of the content being taught."

4. *Learning Experience #4: Use manipulatives.* Elementary classrooms can order plushy neurons from http://www. giantmicrobes.com. These cute "brain cells" can be used to demonstrate neural connections that are made during learning. Primary students particularly like demonstrating brain

activity using these furry brain cells. Kindergarten students can also join hands to demonstrate neural connections.

5. *Learning Experience #5: Use Technology to Show Students' Neurons in Action.* Many videos exist online that demonstrate neural connections. The Cassiopeia Project (http://www.cassiopeiaproject.com) provides free, high-definition science education videos. A video about neurons and their connections can also be accessed through School Wax TV (http://www.schoolwaxtv.com/search/node/neurons). Another good resource is the website Neuroscience for Kids, which is maintained by Eric H. Chudler and was created with the support of a Science Education Partnership Award from the National Center for Research Resources. The site can be found at http://faculty.washington.edu/chudler/neurok.html.

The older the students are, the more details can be added about learning and the brain. For example, once students have an understanding of neural connections, more details can be added. An introduction of dendrites and synapses would be a logical next step. A dendrite is a branch-like projection off of a neuron that receives incoming messages from other nerve cells. A synapse allows a neuron to pass a signal to another neuron. After a discussion or demonstration about creating neural pathways, ask students to complete a formative assessment in order to help you gauge their understanding. Simply give each child a blank piece of paper and ask the students to draw or write about all of the things they learned about the brain. Teachers should provide and review formative assessments to check for understanding. If necessary, work with students who have not conceptualized the idea of the connections of neurons and approach the instruction in a new way.

Sample Learning Task #3: The Brain Is Like a Muscle

"What? You mean I can exercise my brain like a muscle?"—Grade 7 student

Explain to the students that the brain is like a muscle—the more you use it, the stronger it gets. This is usually an easy concept for students to gain, especially when you use a demonstration process like the following:

- Show students a 2-pound hand weight. (Older students may want to use a 5-pound weight.) Ask a student to demonstrate how someone might use this weight to exercise. Ask the following question: "If I ask _____ to exercise everyday with this weight, after a lot of practice what will happen to his arm muscle?" Actual student responses I've heard have included: "He will get stronger," "He will make a strong muscle," and "It will get easier to do." Explain to the students that the more he practices using the weight, the easier it gets. Ask students why this will happen. Students may answer with something like, "Because he practiced every day, he learned how to do it." Continue to question students, "If he wants more of a challenge and wants to continue to build more muscle, what should he do? "

- Then, show students a 3-pound (older students may want to use a 10-pound weight) weight and hand it to the student who is giving the demonstration. Ask him how the weight feels compared to the 2-pound weight. Acknowledge that it is heavier, but with practice, it will become easier to lift. The teacher could further explain the concept by using an example of something students learned earlier in the year and comparing it to something they are learning now. One first-grade student explained it this way: "The lighter weight is like when you learned to count to 10. You practiced until it became easy. The heavier weight is like learning to count to 100! It is a little harder, but if you practice, it becomes easier."

- Ask students to think about how practicing with two different-sized weights is like a brain. Explain that we need to keep trying to learn new things to help our brain get really strong! The neurons make more connections and make our brain stronger just like arms make more muscles from the weights. Tell students, "So even when we face something really hard or challenging, think about all of those new connections your brain is making and how much stronger it is getting!"

You may also want to incorporate the use of the book, *Your Fantastic Elastic Brain: Stretch It, Shape It* by JoAnn Deak, when you're explaining these concepts to elementary students. This book explains the various functions of the brain, how it grows and connects, and what the different parts of the brain look like and do.

After the demonstration, conduct a formative assessment by asking students to recall everything that they have learned about the brain so far. Chart their responses. The main ideas you will want to capture include:

- Your brain can grow and get stronger.
- Neurons in your brain make new pathways or connections when you learn.
- Your brain is like a muscle.
- Exercise (learning and embracing challenge) is good for your brain.
- When you learn something that is at first challenging, keep practicing! This helps your brain get stronger.

Sample Learning Task #4: Taking Care of Your Brain

Explain to the students that it is also very important that your brain gets enough sleep. Studies have shown that lack of sleep affects memory and increases the time it takes to perform certain tasks. Have each student generate a plan that will make sure that he or she gets enough sleep each night.

Older students can research foods that are considered super brain foods. For younger students, explain that certain foods also have an effect on the way the brain functions. Ask students if they know of any foods that are super brain foods. Using picture or plastic foods, show students a few of the best brain foods. One at a time, reveal and discuss the following: eggs, fish, nuts, berries, and bananas. It is important to note that students should eat these foods, as well as other healthy foods, routinely, not just on the morning of a test! As one fifth-grade student announced after this discussion, "Before my test tomorrow, I am going to have a crab omelet with blueberries, bananas, and nuts on the side!" Such comments are a great way to show the importance of taking care of your brain at all times. Point out that it is also important for our brain to drink lots of water and stay hydrated.

Explain to students that physical exercise can also increase brain power. Exercise sends a higher level of oxygen to the brain. This extra oxygen makes the brain more alert. When people exercise on a regular basis, they typically can increase their ability to remember new information and will do better academically.

Sample Learning Task #5: Collection Strategy

In this learning task, a collection of objects assembled around a specific concept is used to help students develop classification strategies, analyze attributes of objects, and discover relationships between items. This strategy is based on Jerome Bruner's Concept Formation model. It is also a powerful tool for developing critical thinking. There are two kinds of collections, *serial* and *revealed*. In a revealed collection, all objects are displayed at the same time. If the common link between the objects is obvious, a revealed collection works well. The focus would be on finding similarities and differences within the group. A set of toy animals or models of transportation that share a connection would make an appropriate revealed collection. A serial collection is used when items are displayed one at a time. After each item, the teacher records students' predictions on index cards as to what the common concept might be for all objects in the collection. With each item that is presented, remove the cards with concepts that no longer work. The last item in this collection is the validator. The validator should help solidify the common concept of the collection. It is possible that many ideas remain that could work to describe the concept presented, that is fine. Just share with the students what you were thinking of. Perhaps they can think of some additional items that would fit in the collection.

When doing this task with students, I like to present the following items in the collection:

- dollhouse bed, pillow, or another symbol of sleep
- toy bike, skate, ball, or an athletic shoe to represent exercise
- banana
- bottle of water
- nuts (picture or plastic if there are allergies)
- egg
- fish (plastic or a picture)
- a science book
- a picture of a school or something to represent a classroom

The common concept that is being formed is "things that are good for your brain" such as sleep, exercise, brain foods, water (hydration), reading, and learning. After the collection is complete, debrief the process of the collection by asking students, "After I took out each object, what were you thinking/what was your brain doing?" Let students know that they just exercised their brains and made it stronger by coming up with all of these ideas (point to category cards). Explain to the students that it does not matter if an idea was the same as the teacher's; they made their brain stronger just by thinking about the connections among the items in the collection!

Review with the students all of the different ways that we can help ourselves become smarter (point to the collection). Tell them, "It is important to always believe that if we try hard, our brain can grow." Discuss the meaning of the word *effort* and ask students to share specific examples of the ways that they put forth effort.

Introducing Growth Mindset Terminology

After completing some or all of the preliminary lessons to build students' knowledge of how their brains work, you're ready to introduce them to the ideas behind what makes a growth mindset. Explain to the students that if we always believe that with effort and persistence we can learn and become smarter, then we will have a growth mindset. Show students the Growth Mindset Poster found in Figure 20.

After students understand what growth mindset means, introduce them to the concept of a fixed mindset. Tell students,

> Sometimes, people do not believe that they can get smarter with effort. These people have a fixed mindset. So if you hear yourself saying, "I am not very good at math or reading or sports," that is a fixed mindset. Instead say: "Math is sometimes hard for me so that means I need to always try harder and practice to make my brain stronger in math."

Using direct examples of the types of things people with a fixed mindset tell themselves (like those shown above) is very helpful for students to understand when they may have had a fixed mindset about a task or event in the past. Encourage students to think about examples of growth and fixed mindsets in their own lives and in the lives of the characters in books, movies, and TV shows they enjoy.

Figure 20. Growth mindset poster.

Next, share with the students that they want to always strive to have a growth mindset. Tell them:

> Sometimes we feel like we can't learn something new like a new video game or how to work a new cell phone or how to speak another language, but then we can remind ourselves to have a growth mindset and realize that if we stay motivated, practice, and try very hard we can learn to do almost anything! In our classroom, we will be working toward having a growth mindset classroom every day. Sometimes I may point to our growth mindset poster to remind you to persevere. Each one of us will always persevere, never give up, and remind ourselves that we need to embrace challenges.

Teaching Perseverance Through Literature

A very effective way to teach perseverance is through literature. Identify and discuss books that demonstrates perseverance, persistence, and effort:

- *The Little Engine That Could* by Watty Piper—After a class discussion about the book, pose this question, "What if the Little Engine decided that he couldn't instead of could, how would the story change?" "What would happen if he said 'I don't think I can' instead of 'I think I can'?"
- *Wilma Unlimited: How Wilma Rudolph Became the World's Fastest Woman* by Kathleen Krull—This is the story of runner Wilma Rudolph. Focus first on the word in the title, "Unlimited." Ask students to predict why the author chose the title. Then, after the book is read, discuss the title once more focusing on Wilma Rudolph's perseverance.
- *Amazing Grace* by Mary Hoffman—Grace wants to play Peter Pan in the school play but is facing resistance; discuss what Grace does to persevere.

- *Gifted Hands: The Ben Carson Story* (Kids edition) by Gregg Lewis and Deborah Shaw Lewis—The real-life story of a boy who went from "class dummy" to brilliant pediatric neurosurgeon. Discuss how Ben Carson persevered to achieve his goals.

Games That Build Perseverance

Through the Critical Thinking Growth Mindset project discussed in Chapter 4, it was discovered that when students engage in reasoning games that grow more complex as they play, they build perseverance for learning tasks. Games made by Thinkfun that progressively grow more challenging, thus building perseverance, include ShapeOmetry, Chocolate Fix, Brick by Brick, Shape by Shape, Rush Hour, Swish and Swish Jr., and Block by Block. It is amazing to witness students who typically give up, persevere and try to get to the next level of challenge. These can be easily justified for classroom use for several reasons. The first is that perseverance is one of the Common Core State Standards for Mathematical Practice: "Make sense of problems and persevere in solving them." Another justification is that these games also build reasoning processes. They can be used as centers or anchor activities and always be available before and after school, as well as during indoor recess time for elementary students.

Facing Failure

One of the areas where students struggle is with the idea of failure. This can be particularly hard for gifted students, perfectionists, and those students who live with strong parental pressure to succeed. Whenever possible, take opportunities to discuss the value of failure.

Asking students to analyze a scenario, quote, or movie clip can be an effective way to engage students in a discussion about the value of failure. For older students, analysis and interpretation of a quote such as Maya Angelou's "You may encounter many defeats, but you must not be defeated. In fact, it may be necessary to encounter the defeats, so you can know who you are, what you can rise from, how you can still come out of it." can serve as a vehicle to begin a critical discussion or debate about the value of failure.

Younger students can be shown a film clip and become engaged in discussion. As mentioned earlier, there is a scene in Disney's *Meet the Robinsons* movie where Lewis creates an invention that combines peanut butter and jelly and it fails. (Search "Meet the Robinsons Failure Scene" on YouTube.) It is effective to stop the video clip right after Lewis buries his face in his hands and apologizes for the failure of his invention. Students can then be asked some of the following questions:

- How does the boy react to the way his invention worked?
- Why do you think he reacts this way?
- What do you think he will do next?
- If you were the boy, how would you react?
- How do you think the adults in the room will react to this situation? Why?

Continue to show the rest of the clip where the adults happily yell, "You've failed! From failure, you learn, from success . . . not so much." Continue engaging the students in discussion:

- Why did the adults react this way?
- What does it mean when they say "From failure, you learn, from success . . . not so much."? Do you agree with this statement? Why or why not?
- Think of a time when you have failed at something. It might be schoolwork, learning to play a musical instrument, making a clay pot, ice skating . . . anything. (Give students an opportunity to think.) Now think about how you reacted to that failure. Did you give up? Try again in a different way? Try again the same way? Get angry? Cry? Celebrate?
- Let's brainstorm some ways that we can react in a positive way to failure. What are some things we can reflect on or ask ourselves when we do not succeed?

After this class discussion, continue to revisit the reflective aspect of reacting to failure throughout the year. This theme can be incorporated in writing assignments, debates, or analysis of characters, historical figures, and scientists who have failed. This learning experience can really make an impact with some students, who gain encouragement from seeing how effort and hard work can eventually pay off. In addition to discussion about the famous failures listed below, ask students to assume the point of view of the person involved in the failure. Some students may be willing to role play. For example, give the students a scenario that is similar to the following: "You are a scientist whose job is to invent the strongest adhesive possible, but instead, you discover that you have developed a reusable adhesive. How would you react?"

Some examples of famous failures include:

- R. H. Macy: The founder of Macy's department store failed at seven previous business attempts.
- Colonel Sanders: Harland Davis Sanders' famous chicken was rejected 1,009 times before a restaurant accepted it.
- Thomas Edison: He conducted experiments on his concepts 9,000 times before he created the lightbulb.
- Post-it® Notes: A scientist at 3M Company was working to create a super-strong adhesive; it was a failure. Instead, he accidentally made a reusable, pressure sensitive adhesive that later was utilized in sticky notes.
- Chocolate Chip Cookies: Ruth Wakefield, owner of the Toll House Inn, was trying to make her chocolate cookie recipe and discovered that she was out of baker's chocolate. She decided to take sweet chocolate and break it into little pieces, adding them to the cookie dough and thinking that they would melt while they were baked. Instead, the little pieces stayed together. She did not have her chocolate cookies in the end, but discovered the chocolate chip cookie through this failure!

Analyzing Authors and Characters
Sample Learning Task

With your students, brainstorm a list of characters that they have gotten to know through their reading during the year (elementary and middle school level) or brainstorm authors that they have studied (middle and high school level). Record the names on cards and group students in pairs or triads. Each group will be given a card with the name of a character or an author. (This is a great time to do some very subtle differentiation by giving more complex character or author cards to students who embrace challenge.) Each group will analyze the character or author's actions/words/written word through a growth or fixed mindset lens. For example, some second-grade characters might include Grace, from *Amazing Grace*, and Alexander, from *Alexander and his Terrible, Horrible, No Good, Very Bad Day*.

An example of an author list for a 10th-grade English course might include Henry Thoureau, Ralph Waldo Emerson, Emily Dickinson, Frederick Douglass, F. Scott Fitzgerald, and Mark Twain. Teachers can write options for authors to study on index cards and hand them out. In pairs or triads, students should discuss what they know about each author and look for additional information as needed. Students will be asked to find evidence in the author's life or his writings that may suggest a fixed and/or growth mindset mentality. They must be prepared to justify their decision with specific evidence. For example a group of students might share:

> We think that Frederick Douglass has a growth mindset for many reasons. A specific example of how he valued effort and persistence can be found on page 58 of *Narrative of the Life of Frederick Douglass* where he explains the process of how he learned to read and write in a very nontraditional manner by copying letters that were marked on timber as well as other innovative ways. He states, "Thus after a long, tedious effort for years, I finally

succeeded in learning how to write." Other examples of a growth mindset in Frederick Douglas' life include . . .

After each group states their argument, cards should be classified into three possible groups: Fixed Mindset, Growth Mindset, and Both Fixed and Growth Mindset. Students can then look at the categories and possibly begin to make some generalizations about authors, time periods, literary philosophies, and movements in relation to a growth or fixed mindset.

A similar task can incorporate video clips of real-life or movie characters into the classroom by using clips similar to those in Figure 21. Have students discuss what they see in the film clips and classify the characters' reactions using a chart similar to the one created for the author studies.

Concept Placemats

The concept placement strategy was inspired by the concept formation model. It is similar to a collection, only it typically builds a more abstract concept and uses only one piece of paper or one projected slide or flipchart. A concept placemat can be developed easily using a computer and clip art, the more challenging part is deciding what images will be used to communicate the concept.

Concept formation relates to making connections, seeing relationships between items of information, and defining a concept from them. Concept formation is a key skill required for learning of new ideas. Is there a concept based on a content area that is being studied that you would like your students to form using images? Choosing a more abstract concept works best. For example, "relationships" works better than "pets." Some other guidelines for developing concept placemats include:

- Once you choose a concept, brainstorm ideas about what kinds of images might represent that particular concept.
- If you develop the concept placemat with the computer, open a word document, and add images. Insert pictures

Title	Summary	Video Clip
Facing the Giants	After missing a field goal kick, David's father tells him that he won't make the kick unless he believes in himself.	http://www.wingclips.com/movie-clips/facing-the-giants/accept-defeat
The Ron Clark Story	After his class performs poorly on their tests just before the state exams are taken, Mr. Clark gives his students a lesson on believing in themselves.	http://www.youtube.com/watch?v=zHMmvD47rX88&noredirect=1
The Rosa Parks Story	A girl in Rosa's class questions why they need to learn if all they will end up doing is serving White people.	http://www.wingclips.com/movie-clips/the-rosa-parks-story/no-one
Pursuit of Happyness	Interview of Chris Gardner. Watch for verbal and nonverbal evidence of fixed and growth mindset on both sides of the table.	http://www.youtube.com/watch?v=gHXKitKAT1E End the clip as soon as the interview is over.
Failure	30-second Nike Commercial	http://www.youtube.com/watch?v=45mMioJ5szc

Figure 21. Suggested mindset video clips.

using clip art or images found online. Three to six images are usually enough to build a concept.)

- In the middle of the concept placemat, place a text box that says, "Find pairs of objects that share a common concept. Find three objects that share a common concept. What concept do all of these images have in common? Be prepared to justify your thinking."

Specific suggestions for concept placemats to create are included below.

Next, within an instructional sequence, determine how the placemat will be used: As a preassessment or formative assessment? Activator? As a vehicle for learning new information? As a springboard to a discussion? The possibilities are endless.

Ask students to look at the placemat quietly. Give everyone a set time (2–3 minutes) then ask for ideas (otherwise the "quick thinkers" dominate) using questions similar to these:

- Who can find two things that are the same in some way? (Take all student responses. During this time observe/listen for unique connections between the images.)
- Who can find three things that are the same in some way? (Take all student responses. During this time observe/listen for unique connections between the images.)
- Now, let's look for some things that are the same among all of the images. (Take all student responses. During this time observe/listen for unique connections between the images.)
- Let's hear some ideas for adding more things that also share the same concept.
- Let's think about why I might have chosen this concept for our class. What do you think we will be talking about? What do you think we are going to learn about? (This question should ask about the content connection of the strategy).

Concept placemats you may consider developing include the following:

- *Concept Placemat #1: Things That Have Potential.* Images can include: flowers being watered, a solar panel, blueprints for a building, a child with blocks, a young child flexing his muscles, and for older students, a pineapple. The pineapple demonstrates potential because it is often harvested before it is fully grown so that the size is consistent when it is cored, sliced, and fitted into its can. An additional discussion can occur about the potential the pineapple may have if it were allowed to continue growing. Would it be sweeter? Juicier? How large would it grow? Relate the concept placemat and discussion back to the students' own potential. (See Figure 22.)

- *Concept Placemat #2: Neural Networks: Study Habits That Help the Brain Learn.* Images can include: Two students working together (collaborative learning), a mnemonic device such as HOMES for the Great Lakes, a picture of various types of flashcards, a mathematical formula being repeated (repetition), and a child thinking about new learning and applying it to other things. After the discussion of the concept, students can use this to reflect on their own study habits and make plans for improving these habits. (See Figure 23.)

- *Concept Placemat #3: Attention and Concentration: Things That Help the Brain Focus.* Images can include: A plate with foods that represent a good breakfast, an image that represents no TV or electronics, a child sleeping, children playing a sport outside, a student using all of his or her senses: hearing, seeing, smelling, tasting, and touching. Discussion can focus on why these things can help the brain work to the best of its ability. Students can make a plan for improving their own brain function. (See Figure 24.)

Figure 22. Potential concept placemat.

Figure 23. Neural networks concept placemat.

Figure 24. Attention and concentration concept placemat.

Teaching Optimism

An optimistic brain is a happy brain. Neuroscientists have discovered that consistent negative or positive thoughts and feelings can affect brain activity and have an impact on learning. The good news is that you can train your brain to help you become a more optimistic person. It just makes sense that a growth mindset classroom is an optimistic classroom. Some relatively simple routines can be put in place in a classroom that will nurture optimism.

The first is a gratitude journal. Students should be given opportunities several times a week to write in their gratitude journal. They can simply write a list of things they are grateful for or write a paragraph or two about a specific event that they are grateful for. A kindergarten classroom that I was visiting volunteered to share their journals with me. They were to write or draw the things they were grateful for. I saw lots of pictures of toys, video consoles, food and family. I noticed that one young boy drew a picture of a watch. When I asked him why he was grateful for a watch he explained that it was actually his father's watch that had been given to him by his father (the young boy's grandfather). He had found out recently that this watch would someday be his and he realized that this was a very special watch, thus he showed gratitude for something that would happen in his future.

This past Christmas, my 15-year-old daughter decided to give all of her friends a gratitude jar. She decorated each jar and wrote a message asking her friends to take a small piece of paper (which she supplied) and each day write one thing they were grateful for. Then on New Year's Eve they would all get together and count their many blessings from the previous year. Teachers can put a similar process in place in their classrooms. Each day every student can respond to a prompt, like "Something good that happened to me today," "A reason that I have a great life," or "I am grateful for these things today." Students would drop the responses into a personal or communal box. What this exercise does is practice optimism. By asking students to look at the good in every day, they are training their brain to be optimistic. Of course, optimism must be modeled and practiced by the teachers and school staff each day.

Growth Mindset Reminders in the Classroom and School Building

In addition to presenting specific lessons about the malleability of the mind and using online resources, think of ways that the message can be embedded within the content of instruction and the learning atmosphere of the classroom. The following are some visual triggers that can be posted in the classroom or in the school hallways that can be used to reinforce the message:

- Growth Mindset Poster (see Figure 20)
- Pictures of people who exemplify a growth mindset:
  o Elementary classrooms: Walt Disney, Michael Jordan, Oprah Winfrey, Harland David Sanders, Abraham Lincoln, Beethoven, Babe Ruth, J. K. Rowling, Frederick Douglass
  o STEM Classrooms: Thomas Edison, Albert Einstein, Robert Goddard, Bill Gates, Ben Carson
  o English/Reading Classrooms: Agatha Christie, Stephen King, J. K Rowling

- Inspirational quotes that contribute to a growth mindset:
  o "We keep moving forward, opening new doors, and doing new things, because we're curious and curiosity keeps leading us down new paths." (Walt Disney)
  o "You may encounter many defeats, but you must not be defeated. In fact, it may be necessary to encounter the defeats, so you can know who you are, what you can rise from, how you can still come out of it." (Maya Angelou)
  o "Many of life's failures are people who did not realize how close they were to success when they gave up." (Thomas A. Edison)

- o "All of old. Nothing else ever. Ever tried. Ever failed. No matter. Try again. Fail again. Fail better." (Samuel Beckett)
- o "It does not matter how slowly you go as long as you do not stop." (Confucius)
- o "It always seems impossible until it's done." (Nelson Mandela)
- o "Never confuse a single defeat with a final defeat." (F. Scott Fitzgerald)
- o "Once you learn to quit, it becomes a habit." (Vince Lombardi Jr.)

Many ways exist to continue building the growth mindset message in the classroom. The most important element is being consistent with the message. The next chapter offers some ways to maintain a growth mindset culture.

CHAPTER 9

WHAT ARE SOME WAYS SCHOOL STAFF CAN MAINTAIN A GROWTH MINDSET SCHOOL CULTURE?

"I think my head is going to explode from all the neurons connecting in my head!"–Grade 2 student

The importance of continually reinforcing the growth mindset message every day cannot be emphasized enough. Maintaining perseverance and effort is a challenge for some students and they need to be continually reminded that they can achieve success. Specific plans to maintain a growth mindset school culture should be embedded in yearly school improvement plans to ensure that they are monitored. During each staff meeting, at least 15 minutes should be dedicated to discussion about maintaining your school's growth mindset culture. Identify areas of strength and areas that could use improvement.

One aspect of a growth mindset school that is often overlooked is the learning environment in the classrooms. A growth mindset classroom must be a safe place where students do not feel judged and are free to take intellectual risks. A trusting, positive relationship between teacher and student is the heart of a secure learning environment. David Sousa and Carol Ann Tomlinson (2011) discussed the importance of empathy in the classroom as follows:

> Empathetic teachers ask themselves if they would want someone to say or do to them what they have just said or done to a student, colleague or parent. For instance, teachers sometimes try to motivate underperforming students by urging them to "try harder." Although the remark may be well intentioned, the teacher is assuming that the students are unwilling to expend the time and energy necessary to succeed. Consequently, students frequently construe this comment to be accusatory and judgmental. When students feel accused, they are less likely to be cooperative. (p. 20)

The learning environment should also be a fear-free zone. Fear is such an intense emotion that it can shut down cognitive processes and force the brain to only focus on the source of the fear and what to do about it. The fear of making an error or experiencing failure is a big obstacle to learning. As mentioned earlier, some students will avoid experiences that may be too challenging due to fear of failure. A growth mindset teacher should discuss these fears with students and reassure them that they will not be judged if they make mistakes or fail. Teachers can also share their own stories of times that they were afraid to take a risk due to fear. Our environment helps to shape us and a classroom learning environment does as well. "Just as adults are affected by their environments, students are encouraged or discouraged, energized or deflated, invited or alienated by classroom environments" (Sousa & Tomlinson, 2011, p. 31) Also important to note is that it can pose a challenge for students to feel supported in a learning environment where work is either too hard or too easy for them, thus, a differentiated, responsive classroom contributes to an intellectually safe learning environment.

Within the context of instruction, the growth mindset message can also be reinforced. For example, the staff at Maryvale Elementary school in Rockville, MD, are very committed to building a growth mindset school culture. In 2012, the school's principal, Karen Gregory, presented each staff member with a growth mindset T-shirt (see photo below) during preservice week and over a 2-year period, the staff has participated in ongoing professional development about ways to build and maintain this school culture.

Karen Gregory (center) and some of her Maryvale staff members in their growth mindset T-shirts.

On one visit to Maryvale, teachers were asked to look carefully at their curriculum and identify places where they could embed the growth mindset message. This exercise allowed for this staff to take ownership of the message—they looked at curriculum in a new way, through the lens of opportunities to nurture persistence, effort, intellectual risk taking, and perseverance. Figure 25 shows an example of how the staff looked at their current curricula and thought about ways the concept of growth mindset could be incorporated.

Each school should brainstorm "Look Fors" that would demonstrate a growth mindset school and class culture including evidence of a differentiated, responsive classroom. These are prac-

Content Area	Unit, Book, Resource, Topic	Growth or Fixed Mindset Example	Comments, Additional Information
Reading	*Lily and Miss Liberty* By Carla Stevens	Lily demonstrates persistence/effort	Historical Fiction Grade 3
Social Studies	Wampanoag Culture	Analyze the Wampanoag for evidence of a growth or fixed mindset	Grade 2
English	*Good Night Mr. Tom* By Michelle Magorian	Analysis of characters through the lens of a growth mindset	Middle School Historical Fiction WWII
Reading	*Wilma Unlimited: How Wilma Rudolph Became the World's Fastest Woman* By Kathleen Krull	Find evidence in Wilma's life that demonstrates perseverance, motivation and effort.	Grades K–3 Biography
History	Susan B. Anthony was a women's rights activist who spent her entire life working for a constitutional amendment giving women the right to vote.	Susan B. Anthony overcame obstacles and persisted in the face of setbacks.	High School American History

Figure 25. Incorporating mindsets into the content areas at one school district.

tices that should be evident in a classroom's physical and affective environment as well as observed through teacher-student interaction. "Look Fors" for a differentiated, responsive, growth mindset classroom might look like the list in Figure 26.

To work toward a growth mindset school culture is a commitment that all stakeholders must make. Be cognizant of new educators joining your staff and have a plan for getting them on board with your growth mindset goals. Continually monitor and reflect on practices that are having an impact and those that need to be improved upon. Would visitors to your school pick up on the persistence and effort that your students are putting forth? Are more students embracing challenging tasks? Are teachers using language that acknowledges what students do rather than who they are? Are students using growth mindset language and talking about neural connections? Are expectations high for all students?

Look Fors in a Differentiated, Responsive Classroom

Ongoing Assessment
- Preassessment with previewing and analysis is consistently used.
- Alternative challenging opportunities and instruction are provided when proficiency is demonstrated.
- Teachers use formative assessments regularly to find students who are ready for more challenge.
- Opportunities for students to self-assess are used routinely.

Flexible/Fluid Grouping Practices
- Flexible subgrouping is an integral part of programming.
- Anchor activities and/or meaningful centers are used to facilitate management of groups.

Curriculum Compacting
- Teachers enable some students to eliminate and/or take less time to cover material.

Expectations
- Teacher expectations are high for all students.
- Students and teachers believe in the ability to develop intelligence.

Figure 26. Sample list of "Look Fors."

Expectations, *continued*
- Recognition of intellectual potential is not entirely dependent on performance in reading/writing/math. Potential is also recognized through discussion, questions, and responses.
- Teacher provides many opportunities for students to think for themselves.

Questioning
- Students are given many opportunities to respond to and ask higher level questions.

Higher Level Thinking
- Instructional strategies that nurture/promote higher level thinking are imbedded in everyday instruction (concept attainment/formation, interpretation, reasoning, problem solving, evaluating).

Acceleration and Enrichment
- Individuals or groups of students are given opportunities to excel beyond grade-level expectations across content areas.
- Opportunities for enrichment occur through application of and reasoning with content, guest speakers, mentors, and technology.
- Teacher supplements or modifies curriculum to facilitate high-level learning.
- Instruction consists of advanced content and differentiated strategies to reflect the intellectual processes of high-potential learners.
- Above-grade-level materials are available to students across content areas.
- Students are given opportunities for in-depth study/research.

Classroom Environment
- Intellectual risk taking is evident.
- A growth mindset class culture exists.
- Learning stations and/or anchor activities are evident in classroom.
- Room arrangement is conducive to group work.
- A variety of student work samples are displayed.
- A wealth of resources at many levels are available to students.

Figure 26. Continued.

CHAPTER 10

SUMMARY

"If you don't practice, your neural connection will break!"–Grade 2 student

The commitment to building and maintaining a learning environment where expectations are high for all students, responsive instruction is the norm, and where all students value effort and perseverance is well worth the time. Adopting some of the components will incite some change, but in order to have the most impact, a symphony of the following should occur:

- Educators who believe that all students can achieve and be successful.
- Students who have a conceptual understanding of neural connections and believe that with effort and perseverance they can learn, be successful, and grow their intelligence.

- Differentiated, responsive instruction that meets students where they are, giving them what they need, when they need it, and how they need it.
- Critical thinking opportunities that are embedded in curriculum, instruction, and assessment.
- A broadened conception of "giftedness" that is focused on talent development and domain-specific strength, and relies heavily on the word "potential" rather than the word "gifted."

Educators teach students, not curriculum. It is time to meet students where they are, expect the best from all of them and provide opportunities for each and every student to succeed. A growth mindset school culture will most definitely open doors for all students.

On a personal note, several years ago I was deep into the whole malleable intelligence, growth and fixed mindset research and provided many professional development sessions to teachers, parents, and administrators on the topic. It was after one of these sessions that I was approached by a participant who suggested that I write a book about the educational implications of growth and fixed mindsets. She shared that she thought I had a lot to offer educators and had the potential to have a positive impact on children. I thanked her for the nice complement and, well, I hate to admit it, but a fixed mindset mentality sprang right back into my head and I thought, "I could never write a book." About a month later, I heard Carol Dweck speak at the National Association for Gifted Children conference and on the plane ride home, I began this book. This process has not been easy, yes, there were times when I considered giving up (especially when my editor sent back my first revisions—thanks, Lacy) but I persevered. As I write these last few lines, I notice that the laundry needs done, I need to prepare for a presentation tomorrow, the dog needs to be taken out, and my daughter is asking for homework help. Juggling family, a new job, and writing has been one of the greatest challenges of my life, but I did it . . . with lots of hard work and effort. Both you and your students can do whatever you set out to do, too!

RESOURCES

Print Resources

Creating Opportunities to Learn: Moving From Research to Practice to Close the Achievement Gap by A. Wade Boykin & Pedro Noguera

Checking for Understanding: Formative Assessment Techniques for Your Classroom by David Fisher and Nancy Frey

Differentiation and the Brain: How Neuroscience Supports the Learner-Friendly Classroom by David Sousa and Carol Ann Tomlinson

Drive: The Surprising Truth About What Motivates Us by Daniel H. Pink

Enchantment: The Art of Changing Hearts, Minds and Actions by Guy Kawasaki

Fair Isn't Always Equal: Assessing and Grading in the Differentiated Classroom by Rick Wormeli

Fall Down 7 Times, Get Up 8: Teaching Kids to Succeed by Debbie Silver

How Children Succeed: Grit, Curiosity, and the Hidden Power of Character by Paul Tough

How the Brain Learns by David Sousa

Mindset: The New Psychology of Success by Carol Dweck

"Mind-sets and Equitable Education" article in *Principal Leadership* (January 2010) by Carol Dweck

NurtureShock: New Thinking About Children by Po Bronson and Ashley Merryman

Outliers: The Story of Success by Malcolm Gladwell

Spontaneous Happiness: A New Path to Emotional Well-Being by Andrew Weil

The Development of Giftedness and Talent Across the Life Span by Frances Degen Horowitz, Rena Subotnik, and Dona Matthews

The Global Achievement Gap: Why Even Our Best Schools Don't Teach the New Survival Skills Our Children Need—and What We Can Do by Tony Wagner

Teaching With the Brain in Mind by Eric Jensen

Train Your Brain to Get Happy: The Simple Program That Primes Your Gray Cells for Joy, Optimism, and Serenity by Teresa Aubele, Stan Wenck, and Susan Reynolds

Children's Books That Can Be Used to Teach About the Brain or Mindsets

Amazing Grace by Mary Hoffman

The Little Engine That Could by Watty Piper

Wilma Unlimited: How Wilma Rudolph Became the World's Fastest Woman by Kathleen Krull

Gifted Hands: The Ben Carson Story (Kids edition) by Gregg Lewis and Deborah Shaw Lewis

Your Fantastic, Elastic Brain: Stretch It, Shape It by JoAnn Deak

Online Resources

NeuroScience for Kids
http://faculty.washington.edu/chudler/neurok.html

This site includes lesson plans, science fair projects, and memory and learning games. It also has some great brain songs for our young learners ("I've Been Working on the Neurons" and "Home on the Brain"), synaptic tag, and other outdoor brain games.

National Institutes of Health
http://www.ninds.nih.gov/disorders/brain_basics/brain_basics_know_your_brain.pdf

This is a printable book with illustrations for upper elementary to high school students

How Stuff Works
http://science.howstuffworks.com/life/inside-the-mind/human-brain/brain.htm

This site's explanation of the brain and how it works is good for middle school and high school students.

BrainFacts
http://www.brainfacts.org

This site explains neuroscience core concepts and includes lots of resources for teachers.

BrainChildBlog (MindUp)
http://brainchildblog.com/category/mindup

This blog provides many examples of how one school uses the Hawn Foundation's MindUp curriculum, including photos of its students and teachers as they explore the concepts that would be useful for any school as it implements the curriculum.

ThinkFun
http://www.thinkfun.com

This company has tons of games that can be used to help kids learn perseverance and develop reasoning abilities. My favorites are ShapeOmetry and Chocolate Fix, but other good ones include:

- Rush Hour and Rush Hour Jr.
- TipOver
- Tilt
- Block by Block
- Brick by Brick
- Square by Square
- Turnstile
- Swish and Swish Jr.
- Lazer Maze

Giant Microbes
http://www.giantmicrobes.com

You can order stuffed neurons here to help illustrate your lessons on neural connections. Young students love the mini-neurons that come in a petri dish.

Cassiopeia Project
http://www.cassiopeiaproject.com

This site includes many videos about science and the brain.

School Wax TV
http://www.schoolwaxtv.com/search/node/neurons

This site includes videos about neurons.

Anchor Activity Ideas
http://www.anchoractivities.com

This website provides lots of links to anchor activities that can be used in any classroom.

REFERENCES

Boykin, A. W., & Noguera, P. (2011). *Creating the opportunity to learn: Moving from research to practice to close the achievement gap*. Alexandria, VA: Association for Supervision and Curriculum Development.

Blue, L. (2012). Motivation, not IQ, matters most for learning new math skills. *TIME*. Retrieved from http://www.healthland.time.com/2012/12/26/motivation-not-iq-matters-most-for-learning-new-math-skills

Bruner, J. S. (1961). The act of discovery. *Harvard Educational Review, 31*, 21–32.

Dweck, C. S. (2006). *Mindset: The new psychology of success.* New York, NY: Random House.

Dweck, C. S. (2010). Mind-sets and equitable education, *Principal Leadership, 10*(5), 26–29

Edmonton teacher who gave 0s for unsubmitted work fired. (2012, Sept. 14). Retrieved from http://www.cbc.ca/news/canada/edmonton/story/2012/09/14/edmonton-dorval-zero-fired.html

Fisher, D., & Frey, N. (2007). *Checking for understanding: Formative assessment techniques for your classroom.* Alexandria, VA: Association for Supervision and Curriculum Development.

The Hawn Foundation. (2011). *MindUp curriculum: Brain-focused strategies for learning and living.* New York, NY: Scholastic

Horowitz, F. D., Subotnik, R. F., & Matthews, D. J. (2009). *The development of giftedness and talent across the life span.* Washington, DC: American Psychological Association.

James, O. (2008, December 26). Genes don't determine your child's ability. *The Guardian.* Retrieved from http://www.guardian.co.uk/lifeandstyle/2008/dec/27/family-medicalresearch

Jensen, E. (2005). *Teaching with the brain in mind* (2nd ed.). Alexandria, VA: Association for Supervision and Curriculum Development.

Joyce, W., Lasseter, J., Spencer, C. (Producers), & Anderson, S. J. (Director). (2007). *Meet the Robinsons* [Motion picture]. United States: Disney.

Kawasaki, G. (2011). *Enchantment: The art of changing hearts, minds, and actions.* New York, NY: Portfolio/Penguin.

Lohman, D. F. (2002, January 9). *Reasoning abilities.* Retrieved from http://faculty.education.uiowa.edu/dlohman/pdf/reasoning_abilities.pdf

Marshall, P., & Comalli, C. (2012). Young children's changing conceptualizations of brain function: Implications for teaching neuroscience in early elementary settings. *Early Education and Development, 23*(1), 4–23.

Moser, J., Shroder, H., Heeter, C., Moran, T., & Lee, Y. (2011). Mind your errors: Evidence for a neural mechanism linking growth mind-set to adaptive posterior adjustments. *Psychological Science, 22,* 1484–1489. doi:10.1177/0956797611419520

Newman, R. (2008). *Malcolm Gladwell talks about his new book, Outliers: The Story of Success.* Retrieved from http://money.

usnews.com/money/careers/articles/2008/12/01/malcolm-gladwell-talks-about-his-new-book-outliers-the-story-of-success

Olszewski-Kubilius, P., & Clarenbach, J. (2012, October). *Unlocking emergent talent: Supporting high achievement of low-income, high-ability students.* Washington, DC: National Association for Gifted Children. Retrieved from http://www.nagc.org/uploadedFiles/Conventions_and_Seminars/National_Research_Summit/Unlocking%20Emergent%20Talent%20FULL%20No-Tint.pdf

Palmer, B. (2011). How can you increase your IQ? *Slate.* Retrieved from http://www.slate.com/articles/news_and_politics/explainer/2011/10/increasing_your_iq.html

Perez, A. B. (2012). Want to get into college? Learn to fail. *Education Week, 31*(19), 23.

Pink, D. H. (2009). *Drive: The surprising truth about what motivates us.* New York, NY: Riverhead.

Renzulli, J. S., Smith, L. H., & Reis, S. M. (1982). Curriculum compacting: An essential strategy for working with gifted students. *The Elementary School Journal, 82,* 185–194. doi:10.1086/461256

Schonert-Reichl, K. A., & Lawlor, M. S. (2010). The effects of a mindfulness-based education program on pre- and early adolescents' well-being and social and emotional competence. *Mindfulness, 1,* 137–151. doi:10.1007/s12671-010-0011-8

Schonert-Reichl, K. A., Oberle, E., Lawlor, M. S., Abbott, D., Thomson, K., Oberlander, T., & Diamond, A. (2011). *Enhancing cognitive and social-emotional development through a simple-to-administer school program.* Manuscript submitted for publication.

Silver, D. (2012). *Fall down 7 times, get up 8: Teaching kids to succeed.* Thousand Oaks, CA: Corwin

Sousa, D. A., & Tomlinson, C. A. (2011). *Differentiation and the brain: How neuroscience supports the learner-friendly classroom.* Bloomington, IN: Solution Tree Press.

Sousa, D. A. (2009). *How the gifted brain learns.* Thousand Oaks, CA: Corwin.

Subotnik, R. F., Olszewski-Kubilius, P., & Worrell, F. C. (2012). A proposed direction forward for gifted education based on psychological science, *Gifted Child Quarterly, 56,* 176–188.

Tomlinson, C. A. (2001). *How to differentiate instruction in mixed-ability classrooms.* Alexandria, VA: Association for Supervision and Curriculum Development

Tough, P. (2012). *How children succeed: Grit, curiosity, and the hidden power of character.* Boston, MA: Houghton Mifflin Harcourt.

Wade, J. F. (2012, July 6). Editorial. *The Daily Bell.* Retrieved from http://thedailybell.com/4055/Joel-F-Wade-Build-a-Growth-Mindset

Weil, A. (2011). *Spontaneous happiness: A new path to emotional well-being.* New York, NY: Little, Brown.

Weiner, B. (1974). *Achievement motivation and attribution theory.* Morristown, NJ: General Learning Press.

Weiner, B. (1980). *Human motivation.* New York, NY: Holt, Rinehart & Winston.

Willingham, D. T. (2008). Critical thinking: Why is it so hard to teach? *Arts Education Policy Review, 109*(4), 21–32. doi:10.3200/AEPR.109.4.21-32

Young, A. (2011, December 12). *On "Rethinking giftedness and gifted education": An interview with ADTP faculty director and talent development researcher Frank Worrell.* Retrieved from http://atdp.berkeley.edu/on-rethinking-giftedness-and-gifted-education

SAMPLE TRAINING PLAN FOR STAFF GROWTH MINDSET PROFESSIONAL DEVELOPMENT

Outcomes

By the end of the professional development participants will be able to:

1. Define the fixed and growth mindset theories.
2. Discuss the research of Dr. Carol Dweck's work on Mindset theory. Dr. Dweck asserts that intelligence is a malleable quality, a potential that can be developed.
3. Reflect on their own "mindset" about student learning, intelligence, and effort.
4. Explore how student praise and feedback influences student's mindset
5. Explore ways to teach students about the brain and how they learn
6. Plan for next steps in building a growth mindset class culture.

Mindsets in the Classroom

Pre-Professional Development Planning

At each table have a folder with copies of the PowerPoint or Flipchart, "My beliefs about intelligence" paper, envelopes for each participant, and the *Mindsets and Equitable Education* (Dweck, 2010) article. In addition, set up four stations with anchor activity folders with alternate articles about growth and fixed mindsets.

Time	Content	Resources
5	**Welcome/Outcomes** Review outcomes and agenda Ask participants to post any questions that they have on the chart "bin" as the day progresses. Facilitator will make every effort to discuss "bin" items.	• Flipchart or PowerPoint with outcomes • Chart paper and sticky notes for "Bin"
5	Inform participants that in a few minutes they will read an article that discusses one aspect of equitable education. The author, Dr. Carol Dweck, describes two sets of beliefs that people have about intelligence. On the paper that says "My beliefs about intelligence . . ." teachers will write down a statement that summarizes answers to the following: • What were you taught about student intelligence? • What do you believe about student intelligence based on your own observations? When they are done, they should put the paper in the envelope, seal it, and write their names and date on the front. The facilitator should collect these and save them for the last professional development session so the participants can note if their beliefs have changed in any way.	

Time	Content	Resources

10	As they read the article, "Mind-sets and Equitable Education" by Carol Dweck, from *Principal Leadership*, have participants use a highlighter to identify interesting or new information.
	
	Tell them, "Write down your initial thoughts/feelings about what you just read. If you finish the article or have already read the article, please choose an alternative reading that can be found in the anchor activities "folder."
		• Copies of
		• "Mind-sets and Equitable Education" article
		• Highlighters
		• Anchor activity folder with recent articles or the following:
		  o *Even Geniuses Work Hard*, Carol Dweck
		  o *Mindsets and Gifted Education: Transformation in Progress*, Matthews and Foster

20	Discuss the article. You may use the following questions as discussion starters (ask participants to think about life outside of school): • In what areas do they think you have a fixed mindset? • A growth mindset? Facilitator should share a personal experience that demonstrates a fixed mindset; for example: • I have a very fixed mindset when it comes to technology . . . in fact, my family gave me an electronic tablet as a gift several years ago, and I wasn't sure that I wanted to keep it. I felt that learning how to operate it would be impossible for me because I do not have a talent for technology. Since getting into this research, I have realized that with effort, I can learn to do anything—I just have to be willing to put in that effort. At your table, choose one of the following questions to discuss: • Do we, as a society believe in a growth mindset? Why or why not? • Is this what we were taught? Or how we were taught? • For some of us, this is a challenging concept to believe in. Why?	• PowerPoint with questions or handout with questions

Time	Content	Resources
5	**Why Now?** Discuss the following ideas with participants: • We continually learn new things about the brain and how people learn and react to situations and relationships. • Fifty years ago if you had a toothache, how would the dentist "fix" it? • How will this new learning have a positive impact on our students?	
30	**How Do We Praise Our Students?** Ask participants to think of some ways that parent and teacher praise can influence the formation of these mindsets. At tables discuss some specific examples of praise that may manifest a fixed mindset. Tell participants: • Every word and action sends a message. It tells children how to think about themselves. It can be a *fixed mindset* message that says, "You have permanent traits and I'm judging them." For example: "You are so smart." Ask participants to come up with other examples that demonstrate a fixed mindset. Record responses on chart paper divided into two columns: Fixed Messages and Growth Messages. Tell participants: • It can be a growth mindset message that says: "You are a developing person and I am interested in your development," "You put a lot of effort into that and it shows!" Ask participants to come up with other examples that demonstrate growth mindset praise. Record responses on the chart paper.	• Chart paper with two columns: Fixed Praise and Growth Praise

Time	Content	Resources

45–60	**Learning and the Brain**
	Discuss the brain with participants:
	• Research over the past few decades has expanded our understanding of the brain's capacity to develop new ability. The brain has great capacity to develop through exercise at the right depth and challenge level. This is the condensed version of how the brain works:
	  o The brain is made up of a network of neurons.
	  o When we learn something new, neurons make connections to each other.
	  o When we practice, put forth effort, and persist, these neural connections become stronger and the brain becomes denser.
	  o The rate of density depends on how much the brain is stimulated and actively used.
	  o We become smarter when we learn new things!
	
	Demonstrate neural connections using thread (a weak understanding), string (on the way to mastery), and a rope (mastery).
	   Ask for 3 to 5 volunteers to be neurons. These volunteers can hang a paper neuron around their neck.
	   Ask the group neurons if someone could share something new that they learned recently (e.g., knitting, golfing, or the Common Core State Standards).
	   For illustrative purposes, we will choose Sara's response. Sara shared that she is just learning about the Common Core State Standards (CCSS). Announce that this group of neurons now represents part of Sara's brain.
		• PowerPoint
		• Thread
		• String
		• Rope
		• Five neurons cut from card-stock (or plushy neurons), put on a necklace string for participants to hang around their neck

Time	Content	Resources
	Learning and the Brain, *continued*	

Learning and the Brain, *continued*

Take a thin piece of thread and ask two of the neurons to connect using this thread. This thin connection will represent Sara's new learning of the CCSS She is just beginning to learn about them, so this is a weak connection.

Ask Sara if there is something that she has learned and that she is getting better at but still might need some practice. In this case Sara may respond with "formative assessment." At that point, two of the student neurons can connect using a thicker connection, a piece of string. This represents a better understanding of formative assessment, but it is not yet at mastery level.

Then propose the following scenario: Let's look at Sara's CCSS connection. It is represented by a thin piece of thread. What will happen to this connection after Sara has more experience learning about and practice with the CCSS? Let's say that Sara reads about, watches videos, asks questions, persists, and puts forth a lot of effort into incorporating the standards into her classroom and is at the point where she can teach others about the standards. How will this connection change? At this point, demonstrate how this thread of a connection is replaced with a strong, thick rope.

What if Sara decides that she is no longer interested in CCSS, wins the lottery, and decides to retire? What will happen to this connection? (It will stay a weak connection or disconnect entirely.)

Time	Content	Resources

	Learning and the Brain, *continued*
	 Ask participants to think of a time when they felt frustrated learning something new. Ask them to visualize their neurons making stronger connections every time they push through the challenge and master new learning. Think about these neural connections when you are faced with a challenge. Once you build a strong connection, you have added density to your brain and actually made yourself smarter!
	 Now, discuss student mindset:
	 • Not only is the growth mindset in step with what we are discovering about learning and the brain, but in working with students, the growth mindset is more constructive and produces better achievement outcomes.
	 • Students with a growth mindset:
	    o Are more motivated to learn
	    o Want to work harder
	    o Are less discouraged by challenge
	    o Use more effective strategies for learning
	    o Achieve at a higher level	

15	At your table, discuss some possible actions that you can take in your classroom to begin developing a growth mindset culture. These actions should address ways to: • value effort and persistence, • teach students about the malleability of the mind, and • share growth mindset with students.	

10	**Summary and Evaluation**
	 Have participants complete a paper that asks the following questions:
	 • As a result of today's PD session, I am
	    o thinking...
	    o planning...
		Evaluation Paper:
		 As a result of today's PD, I am thinking...
		 planning...

APPENDIX B

PARENT NEWSLETTER BLURBS

Parent Newsletter Blurbs in English

First Newsletter Installment

One way that parents can really help their children is by carefully choosing the words that are used when they praise them. Every word parents say and action they perform sends a message to their children. These words and actions tell children how to think about themselves. Parents should always praise their child's effort instead of praising accomplishments. The following table includes some examples.

Do Not Say	Do Say
You are really athletic!	You really work hard and pay attention when you are on that field!
You are so smart!	You work hard in school and it shows!
Your drawing is wonderful; you are my little artist.	I can see you have been practicing your drawing; what a great improvement!
You are a great athlete. You could be the next Pelé!	Keep practicing, and you will see great results!
You always get good grades; that makes me happy.	When you put forth effort, it really shows in your grades. You should be so proud of yourself. We are proud of you!

So the next time you are ready to praise your child, stop and think about how to use that opportunity to praise his or her effort instead of accomplishments.

Second Newsletter Installment

In the last installment of [*name of school newsletter*], parents were given suggestions about ways to praise their children. Research suggests that parents should think twice about praising our kids for being "smart" or "talented," because this may foster a *fixed mindset*. Instead, if we encourage our kids' efforts and acknowledge their persistence and hard work, then we will support their development of a *growth mindset*. Children with a growth mindset believe that with effort and persistence they can learn and achieve in school. A growth mindset will better equip them to persevere and pick themselves up when things do not go their way. Parents should also examine their own belief systems. Do you have a growth mindset? Do you believe that with effort, persistence, and motivation your children can achieve their goals?

Dr. Carol Dweck, an educational researcher states,

> Parents should not shield their children from challenges, mistakes, and struggles. Instead, parents should teach children to love challenges. They can say things like "This is hard. What fun!" or "This is too easy. It's no fun." They should teach their children to embrace mistakes, "Oooh, here's an interesting mistake. What should we do next?" And they should teach them to love effort: "That was a fantastic struggle. You really stuck to it and made great progress" or "This will take a lot of effort—boy, will it be fun."

Some parents need to work at having a growth mindset. It takes time and practice, but it is well worth it when you see the difference that it makes in your children!

Parent Newsletter Blurbs in Spanish

First Newsletter Installment

Una forma en que los padres pueden realmente ayudar a sus hijos es escogiendo cuidadosamente las palabras que usan para elogiarlos. Todas las palabras que los padres utilizan y sus acciones transmiten un mensaje a sus hijos. Dichas palabras y acciones manifiestan a sus hijos cómo pensar acerca de sí mismos. Los padres siempre deben elogiar el esfuerzo de sus hijos, en vez de elogiar solamente sus logros. Por ejemplo:

No Diga	Diga
¡Eres un verdadero deportista!	¡Realmente te esmeras mucho y prestas atención cuando estás en el campo de juego!
¡Eres tan inteligente!	¡Trabajas mucho en la escuela y se nota!
Tu dibujo es maravilloso; tú eres mi pequeño artista.	Se nota que has estado practicando dibujar; ¡cómo has mejorado!
Eres un gran deportista. ¡Tú podrías ser el próximo Pelé! (o usando el nombre de otro deportista)	¡Continúa practicando y verás grandes resultados!
Tú siempre tienes buenas calificaciones; eso me alegra mucho.	Cuando te esfuerzas, realmente se nota en tus calificaciones. Deberías sentirte muy orgulloso/a de ti mismo/a. ¡Estamos orgullosos de ti!

Así que la próxima vez que usted vaya a elogiar a su hijo/a, deténgase y piense cómo usar esa oportunidad para elogiar su esfuerzo y no sus logros.

Second Newsletter Installment

En el último fascículo de [*nombre del boletín de noticias de la escuela*], se ofrecieron sugerencias a los padres sobre cómo elogiar a sus hijos. Las investigaciones sugieren que los padres deberían pensar dos veces antes de elogiar a sus hijos por ser "inteligentes" o "talentosos", ya que esto puede fomentar una *actitud fija*. En cambio, si estimulamos el esfuerzo en nuestros hijos, si damos reconocimiento a la perseverancia y al trabajo fuerte, apoyaremos su evolución hacia una *actitud de crecimiento*. Los niños que poseen una actitud de crecimiento pasan a creer que con esfuerzo y perseverancia aprenderán y podrán desempeñarse bien en sus estudios. Una actitud de crecimiento los equipará mejor para tener perseverancia y para levantar el ánimo cuando las cosas no son como ellos desearían. Los padres deberían también examinar sus propias formas de pensar. ¿Posee usted una actitud de crecimiento? ¿Cree usted que con esfuerzo, perseverancia y motivación sus hijos pueden alcanzar sus metas? La Dra. Carol Dweck, investigadora educacional, manifiesta,

> Los padres no deben proteger a sus hijos de los desafíos, errores y luchas. En su lugar, los padres deberían enseñar a sus hijos a amar el desafío. Ellos pueden decir cosas como "Esto es difícil. ¡Qué divertido!" o "Esto es demasiado fácil. No es divertido." Ellos deben enseñar a sus hijos a aceptar los errores, "Ah, aquí hay un error interesante. ¿Qué deberíamos hacer ahora?" Y ellos deberían enseñarles a amar el esfuerzo: "Esa fue una lucha fantástica. Realmente te mantuviste en pie y lograste un gran progreso." O, "Esto va a tomar mucho esfuerzo—pero mira que será divertido."

Algunos padres necesitan trabajar para lograr tener una Actitud de Crecimiento. ¡Eso toma tiempo y práctica, pero realmente vale la pena cuando se nota la diferencia que hace en sus hijos!

ABOUT THE AUTHOR

Mary Cay Marchione Ricci is an education consultant and speaker. She was previously the Coordinator of Gifted and Talented Education for Baltimore County Public School and an instructional specialist in the Division of Enriched and Accelerated Instruction for Montgomery County Public Schools, MD. Mary Cay holds a master's degree that includes certification in gifted and talented education and administration and supervision from Johns Hopkins University, where she is currently a faculty associate in the Graduate School of Education. She completed her undergraduate degree in elementary education at Mercyhurst University. Mary Cay has experience as an elementary and middle school teacher. In 2010, she received an award for state leadership in gifted education from the Maryland State Department of Education.

Mary Cay is also a frequent presenter at local, state and national conferences and has coauthored several articles for *Parenting for High Potential*, a publication of the National Association for Gifted Children. Mary Cay also serves on the CECTAG board of directors.

Her greatest achievement, however, is her three children, Christopher, Patrick and Isabella, from whom she has learned the most.